Bye Bye Baby

SENTIMENTAL JOURNEY
CAN I FORGET YOU
LET'S CALL THE WHOLE THING OFF

Bye Bye Baby

The Story of the Children
the GIs Left Behind

PAMELA WINFIELD

BLOOMSBURY

First published in Great Britain 1992
Bloomsbury Publishing Limited, 2 Soho Square, London W1V 5DE
Copyright © 1992 by Pamela Winfield

The moral right of the author has been asserted

A CIP catalogue record for this book
is available from the British Library

ISBN 0-7475-1123-3

10 9 8 7 6 5 4 3 2 1

PICTURE SOURCES
Page 1: Joan Williams
Pafe 9 *top*: *San Benito News*, Texas
All other photographs from the author's collection

Typeset by Hewer Text Composition Services, Edinburgh
Printed by Clays Ltd, St Ives plc

This book is dedicated to the GIs who said,
'I'll come back for you, honey,' but sadly,
did not live to do so.

In the past few years, many people I have been counselling as they searched for their fathers have said, 'You should be writing about us.' Then I met Mike Petty at the Southampton Writers' Conference in April 1990 and told him what I was doing and this book began to take shape. On behalf of those who wanted to see their plight made public, I thank him.

This work has been assembled from the stories that have been repeated to me, questionnaires and newspaper cuttings. By request, some names have been changed and their locality omitted.

Pamela Winfield, 1991

CONTENTS

INTRODUCTION

My involvement with this search for GI fathers began with *Sentimental Journey* – the story of the GI brides. In the chapter 'Lost and Found', I related how I had helped Christine. She had come to me as a result of a casual remark to my daughter-in-law Dahlia while the two of them were waiting for children to come out of school. From what followed, nearly three hundred 'children' and their American fathers or families have been united.

At the time that *Sentimental Journey* was published, BBC 2 did a documentary on GI brides with a short segment on the children left behind. Letters from people in the same circumstances arrived at the studio. The producer asked me if I could help them. The fact that I had lived in the USA for fourteen years and kept up with many people there, as well as knowing the country well, proved invaluable for what was to follow.

Those letter writers became founder members of the group which would eventually be known by the acronym TRACE. This name was invented by my husband from the phrase 'Transatlantic Children'. He then left it to the members to choose the appropriate last word – enterprise. Thus: Transatlantic Children's Enterprise.

While my writing was no longer based on that period, TRACE soon became extra baggage that I carried with me regardless of what else I was doing. Any new American I met was enlisted as a 'friend' of TRACE, to be added to the relatives, friends and GI brides in the States who were already involved.

By then, the US Embassy, Salvation Army, Citizens Advice Bureau and advice columns in newspapers and magazines had heard about TRACE and were sending enquiries regarding missing American servicemen fathers to us. We even had one trying to find a World War I doughboy who had been attached to a medical unit in Hampshire.

It became apparent that there are a lot of voices needing to

1

be heard. Not surprisingly, they represent as much of a social cross-section as the women who had dated the GIs. Regardless of background or education, all these people share the common goal of wanting to find the American father who holds the other half of their personal history. 'Part of me is missing' is the most constant comment they make on first contact. Tantalisingly, some, at their fathers' insistence, have his name on their birth certificate but, frustratingly, nothing else. However, the very fact he made a claim on them does show that many partings were amicable.

Besides TRACE, there are other groups engaged in this work in various parts of the country. Some people belong to more than one – which is understandable. What one group cannot provide, another might.

Also included in this book are people who have not joined any group, but who by their own initiative have found their fathers. Their efforts may encourage others to follow their lead.

We can only guess at the total number of children the GIs left behind. The figures quoted have varied from 7,000 to 100,000. However, since there was never any official count, details have been blurred; some children acquired English fathers from their mothers' hasty marriages or were adopted at a time when it was unnecessary to pass on all pertinent information.

What is certain is the fact that more than a million GIs were crammed into this country in the run-up to the invasion of France. The US Air Force filled East Anglia. Some of the Army were barracked on Salisbury Plain. Nissen huts began to cluster on tiny patches of land. Tents sprang up in parks. Men were quartered under the racetrack stands in Nottingham and taken in as lodgers in many other towns. Some had to manage in half-finished houses which had been commandeered. Others spread out in stately mansions. The US Navy slept aboard their ships in ports around the coast or were housed in London in style: hotels and apartment houses were requisitioned for them.

Wherever they landed, these GIs took the British by surprise. Very few people had ever met a 'real' American before. In those days, the United States was more remote than Siberia is to the present generation. All anyone knew about Americans had been learned from 'going to the pictures' – the most popular form of entertainment then.

These men spoke with the same fascinating accents as their heroes on the silver screen. They were also totally different from anyone they had ever met before – so smartly dressed it was difficult to differentiate between officer and enlisted men. A great deal of confusion also arose as to who was a soldier and who was an airman since at the start of the war, the Air Force was called the Army Air Corps.

In a country where, up till then, people 'knew their place', these Americans clearly did not. Everyone appeared to be their equal. They treated everywhere they went, grand or simple, with the same irreverence. Girls who had never experienced more than coffee in a café or a fish-and-chip supper were taken to dine at the best restaurant in town. What did it matter that neither she nor the GI had any idea how to deal with the array of silver on each side of the plate? To him, it was just fancy 'eating out'; to her, it was living in style and she was going to make the most of it.

In many areas there was no avoiding these men. As the film *Yanks* graphically illustrates, the GIs swarmed into villages where country girls had rarely met anyone from as far away as London, let alone Laredo, Texas. A social explosion was in the making. This phenomenon will never happen again unless men come down from outer space.

To British women, those GIs represented the glamour, fun and excitement that Hollywood promised. When they began to arrive early in 1942, the country was a gloomy place with everything in short supply. From the dust-covered bombed buildings to wartime bread, everything looked grey. Everything seemed to be rationed and for many British women, that included men. By now the majority of eligible British men had disappeared into the forces and although Saturday night dances continued, the shortage of males left women dancing with each other.

These women included a great number of girls who were just emerging into adult life, largely from single-sex schools. This meant they were not used to associating with boys in the same free and easy manner that the co-educated GI took for granted. The majority of them were virgins and expected to stay that way until they were married. The word 'sex' denoted gender, not intercourse. Kissing a boy was an exciting prospect. Anything more than a fumble, fully clothed, with a boyfriend was too daring to contemplate. Most important of all, only married women were supposed to have babies. The rest knew that unmarried motherhood turned them into social outcasts. This made fear of pregnancy the greatest deterrent and encouraged any single woman, regardless of age, to stay 'pure'.

Abortion was available but it was illegal and highly dangerous. Invariably the information about where it might be procured came from 'a friend of a friend'. If a doctor was involved, unless he had provable medical reasons, he risked being struck off the register. There were a few that did, if they knew the girl. Usually, this would be a local doctor filled with pity and compassion for what this unmarried girl's future would be unless he helped her. These girls had a better recovery rate than the ones who suffered a backstreet abortion.

There were dire warnings about the consequences of 'getting into trouble' which included being shunted off to the Salvation Army homes from which they would emerge as a domestic help. In today's free climate, it is almost impossible to imagine the power that mothers of that generation wielded over their families. Some, having warned their daughters to 'keep themselves "clean" ' until they were married, had no compunction about throwing them out of the family home if they did not.

At that time, there was little privacy available to indulge in much sexual activity. The back row of a darkened cinema, secluded corners of a building, or a cuddle on the common had to suffice for the daring. It was a rare girl who had a boyfriend with a car and most British cars then were so small, they were hardly conducive to sexual gymnastics. Condoms were not readily available. Couples trying for an hotel room also had to appear married.

The war changed some of those basic rules. Unmarried women over twenty were being called into uniform or other aspects of war work which took them away from home for the first time. This gave them unheard of freedom from parental control. So if those friendly strangers asked them out, there was no one asking questions about their background in order to stop them accepting the invitation.

INTRODUCTION

These men not only had the bravado and charm to go to the smartest restaurants, they were also more candid and possibly boastful about sex, bolstered by an ample supply of 'prophylactics' or 'rubbers', as they called condoms. These were readily available at 'supplies'. The men were encouraged to use them but, of course, not everyone did. They had access to roomy trucks and jeeps and barrack beds – if they could sneak the girl past the guards. Also, by now hoteliers would turn the proverbial blind eye after a wave of Yankee dollars.

In reality, these GIs were no more sophisticated than the women. They too had only the yardstick of feature films, most of them American made, with stereotyped British characters who rarely matched the real people they were now encountering. Nor did the quickly made orientation films on 'Living with the British' put over any meaningful message. They contained advice on social and cultural differences relating more to being the friendly ambassador visiting a British family. There was no postscript on dating the daughter of the house or dealing with the camp followers that congregated round the base gates.

By April 1943, the Provost Marshall of the US Army saw fit to issue a booklet: *How to Stay Out of Trouble*. Not every American soldier bothered to read it and in many cases the damage had already been done.

To many GIs Britain turned out to be nothing like the technicolour movies they had seen, but a blacked-out, weary country. Not all of them realised that these dreary conditions were caused by the war. Some saw it more as an illustration of the hardship stories their largely first-generation parents had suffered in the 'old country' before they had departed for America's bountiful shores. The scarcity of goods and lack of vitality about the drab population confirmed that America was indeed the finest place in the world. Few had experience to prove otherwise. For many, the greatest distance they had ever travelled from home had been to their training camps. A considerable proportion were small-town boys, not long out of high school.

A large number of them were determined to stay faithful to wives or sweethearts they had left back home. They chose to occupy their off-duty hours in pursuits unrelated to chasing girls. They helped in charitable work, especially where it involved being with children; became involved with local churches; crowded into pubs or absorbed the culture and history surrounding them. As for the rest, they became a hit with the British female population.

Many were too inexperienced to make value judgements on the women they met. In fact, as one official opined: 'Few could tell a tart from a title.' While the term 'jail bait' was unknown in the UK, sexual intercourse with a minor was unlawful. This made the encounters dangerous when a well-developed and willing girl did not reveal she was under sixteen. Men who had found them responsive, if not truthful, could be savagely punished by their superior officers; a dishonourable discharge could damage plans they had for their future.

Local judgement tended to be one-sided in the female's favour. One report read out in court caused fury when the number of times the couple had had intercourse in the back of the jeep was notated. No one seemed prepared to consider that this could have been by mutual agreement. These women whirled into romances and took chances they would regret as the GIs began to forget that they had come over to fight a war and that there was a likelihood they could be killed.

Some, however, like young William George Chamless, had the sense to consider such a possibility. He was the small-town boy personified – he had never been on a train until he arrived in England. The problem is that no one so far knows which town he came from. His letters to his British sweetheart have been destroyed. His departure for battle was so hurried there was no time to marry, but he safeguarded their baby's future by arranging for her to receive a government allowance. Now all his daughter has to connect her with her dead father is the fact that his name is embossed in gold across the front of a book brought out by *The Times* in 1954: *Britain's Homage to 28,000 American Dead*.

Marriage was usually seen as the solution to an unmarried girl's pregnancy but the GI could be turned down for a variety of reasons. Her father did not always want a 'bloody Yank' in the family and mother did not want her daughter to go off into the unknown, which America still was, especially if she was not yet sixteen.

Since few homes had telephones, the GI either had to take a chance on a possible confrontation with disapproving parents if the girl was confined to quarters, or communicate by letter. The problem here was that although it was illegal, those letters could be confiscated and never seen by the often frantic girlfriend, who was then left feeling she had been deserted.

Some of the girls did not want to marry the GI just because he had made them pregnant. They preferred to take their chances with the difficulties of unmarried motherhood or let the child slide into a place within the family circle. Later, this would often cause much confusion.

The men who did not want to marry the girl were usually able to receive official support. A smokescreen then came down on the destination of his transfer. There were also COs who made arbitrary decisions to tell the girl the man had been killed at his new posting whether he had gone into battle or not. In one case, an officer on board ship connived with a man to perform a 'wedding ceremony' just before departure. This 'bride' did not realise her honeymoon was over before it had begun. By then she was pregnant.

Divorce was still a subject rarely considered, and for this reason few girls would have taken chances with men they knew to be married. Some men, however, failed to disclose that they already had a wife.

At that time, religion played a greater part in the state of marriage – even more so if the man was a Catholic, which to him meant he was married for life. He would, in most cases, prefer to write off his liaison with a British girl as a wartime memory rather than consider a divorce.

This was a time when, on both sides of the Atlantic, regardless of religion, marriage was supposed to be for ever. Such strong beliefs were being strained to the limit by the war. With husbands away, some lonely wives wanted to go out and play. If this adventure ended up with a baby, they were forced into decisions which involved deceit or desertion.

The penance families could extract from their daughters who had 'sinned' was horrific. One girl was banished by her mother without being given a chance to appeal to her father. The mother's fear was that this pregnancy would contaminate her two younger daughters. Those who could gain no support from their parents were faced with a scarcity of places to find refuge. There were large residences like the Victorian mansion in Malvern known locally as 'the naughty girls' home'. Here, unmarried mothers could arrive, have the baby and leave it to be adopted. Such a retreat was only affordable to someone with an above average income.

Alternatives were various institutions which in some cases had rules which went back more than a hundred years. Thus, for a baby to gain entry to the London Foundling Hospital, the mother had to prove she was of good social standing and had fallen on hard times. (A requirement which persisted into the 1950s.) Those unable to qualify had the choice of mother and baby homes run by nuns or other charities – very basic places often operated in conjunction with adoption agencies. Since it was known that prospective adoptive parents preferred girls to boys, these being the days long before scanning, additional stress was placed on the waiting mother who dreaded being turned away with her child because they wanted *no more boys*.

Women who had been in uniform could enjoy a certain anonymity if they discovered they were pregnant – have the baby, put it up for adoption and return to civilian life without anyone ever knowing. Such secrecy could boomerang on the baby. One man who managed to track down his half-sister who had had the pleasure of being raised by their maternal grandparents, found she doubted who he said he was. This leaves him in limbo, so he has turned the search towards the GI father named on his adoption papers.

Those who were dismissed from the services and brought their pregnancy home found sympathy in the same short supply as for any other unmarried mother. If Mum then decided to go it alone with her baby, she received very little help. The National Assistance Board stopped their 'assistance' at too early a stage in the baby's life. Their attitude was that the mother was responsible for her condition in the first place and was therefore responsible for the child's care from the time it was four months old. The only plus was that there were more day nurseries at this time. However, it took a certificate from a doctor to admit a baby under six months of age.

The social climate of that era meant that it took a lot of courage to survive as a mother in an unmarried state. This general disapproval extended to the children. The impact of the word 'bastard' has now largely been dissipated into a piece of slang. In the 1940s it turned children into second-class citizens not only for the public at large but, in too many cases, for teachers at school.

This lack of compassion was intense enough for some children to find that they were not always able to shed their label in adulthood. Some are still pointed out in the villages that were invaded by the GIs. Many say that they don't begin to feel equal or 'whole' until they find their fathers.

> 'The first time I saw you, I knew right away
> that I would love you till my dying day.
> For ever and ever, I'll hear you say,
> "Hi there, honey, what're you doing today?"
> "I'm spending it with you, my love," I promptly
>   answered my man.
> That's if you feel the same as I do,
> that's if you say I can – I will.'

This poem found by Pat K. after her mother died reflects the feelings those British girls had for the GIs who were to change their lives for ever. Her mother loved him so desperately that there was never to be another man in her life who mattered. Pat K. has yet to find her GI father.

ONE

Who's Hiding the Secret?

Usually Mum, by now not easy to equate with a gay young woman without a care in the world. It is possible that the very circumstances of having the child may have made her prematurely old.

> 'When I was a little girl and my mother and I were out walking or sitting on a park bench, she would sing, "Lover come back to me." She never looked at another man throughout her entire life. She devoted it to bringing me up and giving me the best life she could as a single parent in difficult times.'

Having kept her child against all adversity, it does not follow that Mum is prepared to confess who was Dad. This may be due to the fact that those mothers are now a generation apart from today's more liberal view which has removed the stigma of illegitimacy. They still find it difficult to talk about what they see as the most shameful episode of their life. It is preferable to claim they 'can't remember'. This is exasperating to their children who refuse to believe them. Their scepticism is confirmed by the fact that up till mid 1990, one mother insisted all she knew was the GI's first name, town and state – as useless as a locked door without a key. When she finally dredged up his last name, a proper search commenced.

Similarly, a letter which arrived for me in 1990 showed a conscience pricked. The woman finally felt she owed her child the right to know its father but, 'because I had been brought up strict and had misbehaved, I was ashamed to see him again'.

At around this time, I received a telephone call from a man so obviously in shock, he was having difficulty communicating. Eventually, he was able to explain that at the age of forty-five, his mother had suddenly told him that the father he assumed to be his was not in fact his real father. He had been a GI. It is quite understandable that such a deception can leave a person bewildered and hurt. However, looking at it from the mother's point of view, it may have taken her all this time to accept that the child had the right to know the truth. Equally, the reluctance may stem from the fear of losing this child and the grandchildren to the GI who, regardless of earlier circumstances, has equal claim.

Some mothers are determined to carry the secret to their grave or realise too late that they have no right to withhold it. 'There's something I've got to tell you,' said one when she knew she was terminally ill. She was never able to speak again. Others, like the lady who wrote the poem, prefer to leave letters to be found after their death.

Once the discovery is made that there was a GI father, the child may become unsure of what sort of person his or her mother might have been and certainly will not believe it possible that she was a tart or a camp follower. Nor does the child really want to feel they are the result of a one-night stand or any other short-lived situation. I only encountered one person who now lives in the USA who was able to be nonchalant about the possibility that her mother never knew who her father was: 'Could it be my dear old mom fooled around more than once?' Someone else who prefers to be open-minded says: 'I have only heard one side of the story as to why he done a runner. I'd like to hear it from him.' More often they find it almost impossible to perceive mother as someone who didn't even stop to enquire the GI's name; didn't hear it properly; never wrote it down nor communicated with him again. One of the problems was the so-called 'similarity' of the language. For example, those charming American accents were not always distinct enough to differentiate between Mass. for Massachusetts or Miss. for Mississippi, however long the romance lasted. How was a British girl to know that there was a Manhattan in Kansas as well as New York? And although the GI may have enlisted and trained in California, it did not follow that there was where he had grown up and was known.

Rather than confess to being a small-town hick, some of the men preferred to brag that they came from a recognisable large city. If he moved base in the UK or went into the invasion of France and letters were exchanged, APO numbers were used. These did not show anything but the main US services mail distribution centres. This may be why so many women tell their children that their father came from New York. They did not realise this was the main APO for Europe.

If a girl never saw her GI's name written down, she had to guess the spelling. All too often it seemed foreign in a country that was at that time heavily populated with Anglo Saxon names.

Alcohol had to take its share of the blame. These young women could rarely handle, nor knew too much about the strong drink served profusely at GI parties. Up till then, they may have daringly had a shandy or perhaps a port at Christmas. Under the influence of something as unknown as rye whisky, they could have become too drunk to know who had taken advantage of them.

For all these reasons, discussions about 'who was Dad?' can become acrimonious. Margaret A. from Lancashire has run into a wall of words. She has tried all kinds of tactics:

'My mum doesn't understand how I feel; the need I have to know about my dad. She wouldn't answer at first when I wanted to find out about him. Her answers are always the same: "I can't remember, it was a long time ago." I can go in cool and calm, tell her how much I love her and how things won't change – beg her to just give me some information, the slightest thing. Nothing! Another time, I go in mad and crazy, hurtful. Still, whichever way I try, there is nothing but, "It's a long time ago, I've forgotten." Most of the time, it ends with us both crying – me because I am so damn frustrated at her for refusing to tell me anything but his name which she insists is correct.'

This name has a hint of French which, coupled with Margaret's dark skin, suggested she should start her search in Louisiana in the hope that her father is descended from one of the plantations owned by the French before the Louisiana Purchase made it part of America. From there she tried it in every computer system across the States without any luck. It is possible that the name offered has been misspelled, but questions asked around the Welsh village where he was stationed have brought Margaret no further forward:

'I found out from my friends that my dad used to go to my grandmother's house, so it was no one-night stand. If it had been, I think I could understand it and perhaps I would have accepted it better because I wouldn't have gone on so long trying to find him. They all said he used to go back and forth and also how much I look like him, and this I can't handle. I don't know if they tell me I look like him to make me feel better or whether it is the truth. I try to push this to the back of my mind but it flares up every now and again because as long as I am alive, it's in me because it's part of me.'

Another frustrated child says: 'Every time I question my mother, she says I should leave him alone to live his life, as he is now an old man.' Not a very satisfactory explanation for someone who feels that half of her own life is missing. And yet some do begin to realise how terribly poignant their questions are; that their mothers went through a wonderfully exciting romance which has never been surpassed, or that they are intruding on a piece of private history which isn't well remembered and could have been deliberately struck from her mind. A further child recalls her mother's reaction to her questioning: 'It was one of the most unpleasantly emotional visits I have had to endure in many years. She vehemently denied him and screamed that she had only ever had anything to do with the man who later became her husband.'

When Leone W. from Cornwall found a photograph of a US sailor and asked her mother who he was, she was informed briskly that this was her father, but he was dead. After she had grown up and married, a family discussion revealed that her grandmother had been part of the plot to keep the truth from the child. She became very agitated that Leone should now be raking up the past and upsetting her mother: 'We had an awful row and my mum gave me all the photos of my dad and her together, also a label from a parcel my gran [US] had sent containing baby clothes back in 1945.' A letter Leone sent to the address on that label was returned, marked 'unknown'. Nothing more was to happen until she heard about the organisation TRACE.

The most common explanation for a missing father was to say he was dead. Psychologically, it was better to convince oneself that this was what had happened rather than feel deserted. 'My mother had always preferred to think of my father as dead because she said "he always said he'd come back".' This was no brief encounter but the couple had had to meet secretly because her family forbade this young woman to associate with 'Yanks'. This left the daughter with no one to answer questions which might elicit clues to finding her father.

During the war the registration of births did not receive much official scrutiny. Many girls took advantage of the fact that there was a short-form certificate which eliminated the need to name the father. Therefore, it was not until many years later, when a child for perhaps business reasons needed to provide a long-term certificate, a copy of which would be at St Catherine's House, that they would then discover the space for their father's name was blank and that their mother's cover was blown. At this stage, Mum, now perhaps a granny, found it hard to explain a wild and woolly episode from her past.

The war also gave some of the women an alternative way to protect themselves from social condemnation. One could buy a ring and imply there had been a British soldier husband killed in battle. That might have satisfied neighbours, especially if she now lived in a new area, but it did not pass muster with the child asking questions.

Until Jan O. from Northamptonshire needed a full birth certificate for a business venture, she had accepted that her father was a British soldier who had died in the war.

'I discovered not only was he a GI but there was a possibility he was still alive. His surname was very common except for the middle initial which would have provided a wonderful clue if my mum could have remembered his home state. I tried cajolery, threats, even had her hypnotised, but she could tell me no more than the fact he'd been in the Air Force and where he was stationed.

'She'd been in the NAAFI, serving in the canteen. I tried to find some of her friends and couldn't. I examined every US telephone directory I could lay my hands on, searching for names with matching initials. My letters began to be counted in hundreds before one of them reached a family who had lost a brother by that name. Friends of theirs visiting England came to see me but the details didn't match. They still wanted to adopt me into the family, but I refused. It was more important to find my real father.

'Through my investigations, I made contact with a private investigator in Ohio who tried to help but we never got any place until he was approached by a television company for the series *Unsolved Mysteries*. They came over to film and in the interview I said that if my father was viewing and he was broke, I had the funds to bring him over to my home in England where he was welcome to stay. This brought in a large number of letters but none proved to be related. Then, like magic, a lady walked into the TV studio in California and declared she was my older half-sister whom I had mentioned that I knew I had. By then it was late at night here and we agreed to exchange photographs but it took me forever to find somewhere I could receive them on a fax. We finally went to a large hotel in town and they agreed and it was nerve-racking waiting but worth it. There was no mistaking how much alike we were.'

Jan has discovered that her father's wife is in very poor health and there is no way his extramarital adventure in England can be broken to her which means that for the moment Jan cannot meet him. For the present, she is content to have visited her sister, to talk to a brother on the telephone and wait for the appropriate time to meet her father.

Adoption was to prove the best way out for many of these distressed mothers. At that time, it was possible to arrange them privately as well as going through the several societies connected to the homes that took in pregnant, unmarried women. Some preferred to avoid these homes because of the potentially embarrassing questions asked. A private adoption was less stressful for them but could turn out to be a risky business for the child. They had little protection if anything went wrong.

One boy who was adopted privately was fine until he was in his teens. Then, the couple had a natural child and lost interest in him. From then on, everything he accomplished was through his own determination. This may well have been bolstered by his American genes since he has grown up to look like an incarnation of the big, blond GIs who were devastating to many British women.

In the majority of cases, especially where it was official, children did benefit from adoption. This was partly due to the fact that the middle class was the prime group to undertake such responsibility then. Invariably it resulted in these children being raised in a better environment and receiving a superior education to anything their own mothers' circumstances might have allowed. However, adoptive parents could at that time decide whether or not to give the child any details of their birth parents, so few did. And there was little in the way of social workers or counsellors to warn them of the consequences of concealing this kind of information. This was to mean that for many, their true background came as a shock in later years.

The staff involved in the adoptions also neglected to consider the possibility that the papers filled in by the mother listing the reasons why she was handing over her child, together with comments, would be seen in later years. When they became accessible along with the blunt opinions of the mother, they were often distressing: 'The mother of this baby girl is only eighteen and appears to have no feeling for the child and has quite rejected her.' Alternatively, they spoke badly of the father: 'Father failed to keep in touch by correspondence and obviously does not intend to marry me.' 'Father and I had been keeping company for a year. He departed as soon as I became pregnant.' This particular GI was traced to a home and business address in the USA but refuses to respond.

Tina J. from Slough had the good fortune to be adopted by a wise couple which was as well once she read the circumstances of why her mother had to give her up:

17

'I felt sympathy and sadness for her; she had only been nineteen and thrown out of home by her parents . . . I experienced some hostility towards my father because I felt he had abandoned us both. Knowing he was a GI made me begin to understand why when growing up I had had a passion for all things American.'

After finding her mother she had enough details to trace her father: 'I wrote a brief letter to make sure I had the right person. When he responded affectionately, I needed no further encouragement and promptly wrote a fourteen-page letter, giving him thirty-two years' worth of news!'

Twisting the truth could also cause pain: 'It was only when my adoptive mother died and I had to sort out the papers that I saw my natural mother's name in print. She had not died in childbirth as I had been led to believe. I wanted to look for her right away but my adoptive father was alive and had gone through enough at that time.'

Roger G. of Exeter was another one who was not told anything about his background whilst growing up. Then his adoptive mother died and her husband confessed that very soon after Roger had come to them, American visitors had arrived in the area making enquiries. For fear they would claim the child, the couple had turned them away without any information. Such selfish motives were not unique. Little consideration was given then to the child's future feelings or emotional need for a true identity.

To get his full history, Roger had to find his natural mother. He discovered that at the time she had written to tell her GI she was pregnant, he was in the thick of battle. Her letter came back: 'missing, believed killed'. She saw her only solution as having the baby adopted, but at least she kept the GI's details. This included his name and home state which was Massachusetts.

When I was approached for help, I suggested we try the *Boston Globe* which was the leading newspaper in the state.

'It was a long shot and the reporter doubted I had a chance but was willing to do the story. Within twenty-four hours of it appearing, someone who said she was my half-sister came forward. It was a picture of me which accompanied the story that did it. She said it was like looking at a young version of her dad.

'I stayed cautious, afraid it might be a mistake, until we exchanged photographs which I took to my natural mother who confirmed that the one they sent marked "Dad's English girlfriend" was her. In fact it came off the same roll of photographs which she still had.

'I took the next plane to Boston. My father was in a veterans' home, his health fragile from the war wounds which had led them to first assume he was dead. He had been returned to the States badly injured which meant there was a delay before he could try to find my mother and as I now know, when enquiries were made, they were turned away. He never, of course, received the letter which told him he was to be a father.'

Anne R., who also lives in the West Country, was another one taken by surprise. She, like Tina, had caring adoptive parents but admits:

'I did feel different growing up. At first the implications of adoption were lost on me. When I grew older and became aware of the facts of life, it dawned on me that I was in all probability a bastard child. In the 1950s this was something horrendous, at least in the quiet backwater I grew up in; no one wanted to know anyone of such dubious stock – or so I thought. I grew to hate the word adoption and did everything I could to avoid disclosing the fact I was adopted. I well remember the agonies suffered just in case the "best friend" of that time EVER found out! What I had not realised was that in my small town everyone knew I was adopted and just accepted it. But how was I to know that? It wasn't until I was approaching my fortieth birthday that the urge to find my mother became irresistible – triggered off by seeing how much bereavement and loneliness was affecting older people in her age group. My only concern was to make sure she wasn't in need of financial aid, or friendship. Even if she had not wanted or been in a position to acknowledge me, I wanted her to know how much I appreciated what she had done for me and how I understood what she must have gone through. She received me with great joy and thankfulness that I cared to find her.'

The revelation that her father had been a GI came as a great surprise to Anne, but because there was so much else to talk about at that first meeting, they did not discuss this in any detail. Shortly after, Anne's husband who was in the British Navy was posted to America. While she was there, her natural mother died.

This should be a caution to anyone about to embark on finding their natural mother to learn more about a GI father. Don't wait! Get all the details as quickly as you can. This may sound like harsh advice, but what is even worse is to get this far then be denied the final details.

'I didn't feel it was right to put too many questions to her then; I thought we would have many years together. When I came back to England to the funeral I found an aunt there who could supply my father's name. I very soon located someone with that name but he did not reply to my letter. Unable to accept his silence, I continued with my enquiries and found the right pathway again.'

What was to follow resembled a suspense story. Just when her husband's tour of duty in Florida came to an end, Anne learned that her father lived in a northern state. With only a few days left in America, she rushed up for a brief meeting: 'I found I also had a grandma who literally kissed the skin off my face! Later, I managed a longer return visit with my daughter who got to meet her GI grandfather, so we have happy memories to share.' This has assumed even greater importance because Anne's father died at Easter 1990: 'His last words to me the week before was to tell me how much he loved me and to say how thankful he was that I had persevered and found him and made his life complete – what more can I ask for?'

Heather N. of Berkshire wishes she felt the same about the result of her search. She was forty-two when she decided to find her natural mother. Her adoption had not been satisfactory: 'I agonised over the possible consequences to myself, my family and, most of all, my mother. Time was one deciding factor: if I left it much longer, my natural mother may have died of old age. All I knew about my real parents was that they had not married one another.'

Until the 1973 Children's Act, it was illegal to trace a natural mother. Since then many have embarked on what can be a tortuous route.

'After counselling by a social worker, I received my original birth certificate. Tracing my mother was the easy part. She was then contacted by an intermediary from NORCAP (National Association for the Counselling of Adoptees and Parents – this organisation helps adoptees and their natural parents get together). I eventually spoke to her on the telephone then had a letter recalling a few details of my heritage. My mother's rejection and insensitivity gave me an incentive to find my father. He couldn't be any worse, and, besides, I did not feel the emotional need for him, so I felt I wouldn't be hurt again.'

She was, however, taken by surprise to discover that her father had been a GI. 'It was ironic, for the American culture had never endeared itself to me and I have been known to express opinions on the subject. However, my curiosity was doing cartwheels.'

Heather and her husband combined a business trip to America with a visit to the small town where her mother said the GI had lived. There she met someone who remembered her father and was able to give them the name of his best friend from his youth. 'He came to our motel. I showed him my mother's letter and, though he was amazed, he believed, as I did, that she had no reason to lie.'

What may have clinched Heather's claim was the fact that this man was stunned at how much she looked like her father. She learned with great relief that he had never married, so there was no danger of disrupting a family life here. Unfortunately, he was out of the country. Two weeks after her return to England, a letter arrived from him – he wanted to come over for a visit. Sadly, this meeting was not a success: 'Our diverse cultures clashed. I am quintessentially English; he is the embodiment of the "American Dream".'

The problem seems to have been that Heather could not comprehend his state of mind or his pride in what he had accomplished. He was a 'small-town boy made good', which meant nothing to her: 'We still write to each other but we'll never understand each other – it's a dichotomy. Yet I know he is genuinely fond of me.' There are many variations on the theme of clashing cultures and a need on both sides for them to be overcome.

An additional problem as Heather discovered is that the natural mother may have put this episode of her life so firmly behind her that she is fearful that her illegitimate child will disrupt her present life. This can be dealt with in various ways. Some of these newly-found children have been introduced to the rest of the family as long-lost cousins or godchildren. But, however much a counsellor tries to prepare them for rejection, hearing a screaming denial of their existence is difficult to accept. It does appear that mothers who have never married are better able to deal with being found and are usually more thankful. However, at all times, it is advisable to proceed with caution.

After she found her mother's address, Julia G. of Liverpool went to a great deal of trouble to make sure that she would not disrupt her life. First she contacted a neighbour to make sure the woman was not married. In spite of her precautions, when she called, her mother slammed the door in her face. Accepting that arriving unannounced caused too much of a shock (this is always inadvisable), she allowed an interval of six months before returning. This time she was allowed in, 'But my mother insisted that the girl that had turned up earlier wasn't me and would not be convinced otherwise.'

Meeting her natural mother made Julia realise that she would get little help in finding her father but, 'All through my adult life, I used to think and wonder, what flesh and blood am I walking around with?' This was in spite of the fact that Julia had enjoyed such a happy adoption that she did not consider starting her search until both adoptive parents had died.

Her adoption forms proved puzzling. They are an example of

someone guessing a foreign name. No one had considered that a phonetic spelling could change the man's nationality so that ending a last name with an 'e' instead of an 'i' could make a man a Mexican instead of an Italian. 'I couldn't read the writing and had to ask who was the priest who had written the original paper in 1946. All I wanted was this handwriting sorted out.' After she tracked down the priest, she realised that her father had been listed with the wrong surname. Added to that, her research was to reveal he had changed his first name a couple of times. This caused further complications and inevitable delays.

After each setback she took time out to recover, which she now bitterly regrets because by the time she found out where he was, her father was dead.

'I missed him by only five months. I was devastated. If it had been five years, I could have accepted it better. I cried my eyes out. At that point it was the worst thing that had happened to me since the loss of my adoptive father twenty years earlier.'

Some mothers keep the secret but start the search for the father in order to compensate for the guilt they feel about having withheld him from their child. Unfortunately, such actions can deprive the child of that father, especially if the mother's motivation includes thoughts of 'what might have been could now happen'. The GI may well be ready to welcome his child, even grandchildren, but if the package comes complete with the old girlfriend, he is likely to refuse. He may have returned to a wife or a high school sweetheart; in neither case would he necessarily have confessed to unfaithfulness.

Ignoring any of those possibilities, one woman prefaced her letter suggesting that 'we pick up the threads of our friendship'. This ruined the chances of an Oxbridge graduate meeting his father. The man is a lawyer in a New England state. One can assume he is a respected member of a community in an age bracket which adheres to standards which do not include married men rekindling old flames. Whilst he might have managed a meeting which could have dealt with an explanation for this British son, communication with an old girlfriend was out of the question. In spite of numerous attempts, one through an intermediary so that it carried a US stamp, there has only been silence.

Another mother did no better by interfering in a telephone conversation which was a halting explanation between daughter and father. To hasten the process, she grabbed the phone. He panicked and hung up. Short of one abortive attempt to ring his daughter back which was short-lived because someone came in the room, there has been no further communication.

Some mothers have redeemed themselves by subsequently acting with a little more discretion. In one case it led to a 'friend' of TRACE offering to be the intermediary. Eventually, through his efforts, the mother and her English husband took the GI's son over to the US for a grand reunion which included the American wife.

Another one managed a tactful foray into the GI's world on behalf of their child. When she discovered he was dead she had a sympathetic hearing from his sister. This set in motion an exchange of letters between cousins and in May 1991, the following note came to me:

'Linda and her husband have just come back from the States after visiting her father's family. They made them both very welcome and they hope to go back again some time in the future.'

During the writing of this book, several other mothers have smoothed a similar path, enabling siblings there to fill in the picture of their father for the British child.

TWO

Shall We Keep It in the Family?

Not every daughter who brought 'shame' on the family was thrown out. There were alternative solutions. The most dramatic appears to be the family who made a mass exodus from their village to the anonymity of London to make a fresh start away from local gossip. Such a relocation was the ultimate sacrifice since at that time people rarely left their home area by choice. It was only the calls of war work, a house being destroyed by bombing, or evacuation from town to country because of the air raids which displaced the population in war years. If the absorption of the child within the family by the parents of the daughter 'in disgrace' could be accomplished with as little secrecy as possible, the results, it was thought, would be better. It rarely proved that simple.

Single girls who 'gave' the baby to childless married sisters may have felt that this was the perfect solution. Perhaps they did not anticipate the difficulties that would be caused if they stayed around. A natural tug of love could develop leaving the child confused and guilty. Why should he be so drawn to Auntie rather than Mum? Such close proximity could also affect the authority of the aunt-turned-mother and spoil the love they did not necessarily wish to share. Alternatively, if they were willing and encouraged it, the child could still feel disloyal: 'I found my mum's encouragement to give special attention to "Auntie Kay" confusing. I had been told from the start she was really my mother; this never registered with me or perhaps I refused to accept it.'

25

One of the most successful sister swaps in this book benefited the child enormously: 'I knew I was adopted; I loved my new mum and dad. "Auntie" had a terrible husband.' She was to discover this natural mother had done her a great favour because she was not that husband's child. Since he was cruel to his own children, she would have suffered more. She saw she had had a lucky escape, but her adoptive mother tried to make it up to her sister:

'She visited us often and Mum was always saying, "Be nice to Auntie," but when you are growing up, you don't think much about why. It wasn't until "Auntie" fell ill and Mum encouraged me to spend more time with her that I realised the truth. Just before she died, "Auntie" told me who she was and how she had met a GI in Trowbridge, Wiltshire, where they had moved because of the bombing. She was married. The only person who might have known or remembered his name was Grandma who had confiscated his letters that came after and she was now dead. Regardless, I've tried to find him by writing the story of their romance and sending it to loads of American papers. So far I've had no response.'

Carole H. of Cambridgeshire was adopted by her aunt after her mother committed suicide by drinking rat poison. Her search for her father is made even more frustrating by learning that he did send money for her and her mother to join him in the States. It was the family confiscating the fare that led to the girl's final despair.

Being kept in the family did not prove a happy rescue for the child: 'I was sexually abused by my adoptive father for thirteen years. I ran away at fifteen and left home completely at seventeen.'

The aunt who adopted her says she notified the GI of both her mother's death and the fact that the baby would stay with them, but she refused to hand over his last known address nor will she allow any of the rest of the family to fill in details. 'I have learned from the neighbours about the treatment my mother received and it is probably guilt that stops them.'

Carole's daughter was so saddened by watching her mother

try for twenty years to prise something out of these obstinate people that she placed an advert in the local Oxford paper in the hope that it would attract the attention of someone who knew the poor, suffering girl who had been her grandmother. 'The response was amazing; workmates and neighbours rang up. It was a very emotional time for me. Not only to learn about my parents, but one lady sent me a photograph of my mother – she was beautiful.'

This has not made Carole's aunt any more helpful: 'She has refused to hand over photographs of my parents which she had originally promised to do on my 21st birthday.' Even more frustrating is that in spite of the encouraging response to the newspaper advert, the only concrete information Carole has is her father's name and the fact that he worked at the Churchill hospital during the war. She is now trying to locate old records that reveal more details. Without further information she will get nowhere because, again, it is too common a name to provide any other clue.

Some pregnant daughters literally dumped the baby on their parents and left them to sort out the consequences. This could have been their punishment for not allowing them to marry the GI or, alternatively, not seeing the marriage they encouraged as the solution.

However good grandmas are at pretending to be Mum, their age may preclude them from being around too long. In addition, they may not necessarily have the energy to raise an active child which is why, as 'Anna' says, 'I had this old lady looking after me, a doting, devoted grandmother trying to compensate for her own widowhood and the loss of a son in the war. My mother was a beautiful princess who appeared in and out of my life like a tapestry being woven.'

Anna's mother had been let down by her GI and soon married an old sweetheart who took her off to live abroad. 'I was always going to join them, but it never happened.'

When 'Anna' was twelve, her grandmother died. Her mother came back for the funeral and was supposed to take her daughter off to a new home, but by then she had other children who did not know about 'Anna' and she preferred to keep it that way. Another sister was appointed the child's guardian and 'Anna's' mother continued to make sporadic visits to 'the family' in England. On one of those occasions 'Anna' confronted her to demand to know more about her father: 'She couldn't understand why I wanted to dig up the past and gave me the wrong name. I adopted a bit of subterfuge and finally found the correct one and that he had lived in Georgia.' There, she was informed by the Veterans' Administration office that he had died. She did, however, learn that he had two other children. Since she was cut off from her mother's children, she was desperate to find them.

Then, in May 1991, I received a long letter. 'I feel someone should pinch me.' The family had found her. In a series of telephone calls, she talked to a brother in Georgia who had contacted two others, a sister in Florida, from whom she discovered how closely their lives had run parallel, and another brother in Georgia who told her that their father had told each of his children what had happened when he was in England. 'Anna' is one of seven siblings and is making plans to visit them. 'This could be the beginning of a whole new chapter, and just when I'd given up hope of finding them.'

If a young mother had died in childbirth, a not uncommon phenomenon in the 1940s, it might be only one grandparent who wanted to keep the baby. This left the child growing up with unexplained resentment from the other one.

Grandmas who saw a new lease of life in adopting the title 'Mum' and taking over the baby, could later fight to retain it by foul methods. They would confiscate letters arriving from the GI wanting to claim his child or keep him at bay by concocting frightening stories about him to tell the child. One can be kind and assume in some cases such lies were a defensive measure to explain away the apparent lack of morals exhibited by the unmarried mother. One way or another, it was the grandparents who proved to be the cause of the greatest confusion in these family matters, leaving the children with the problem of sorting out who they really were – often too late to do much about it.

Howard B. of Nottinghamshire was one such victim:

'I used to call my gran "Mum" but never called my grandad "Dad". I came home from school one day and asked my gran

why I had not got a dad like the other boys. I never got a
straight answer. It was some time before I found out that my
"auntie" was my mother. After my mother's younger sister told
me that, I went straight to my mother and confronted her. She
admitted that she was my mother. I felt resentment, let down,
unsure of myself. I went through a difficult teenage life calling
her names in frustration because she could not help me or tell
me how to find my father.'

He was to discover that his grandmother had driven the GI
away before he was born and hidden the letters that followed.
Determined to get to the bottom of his family history, Howard
searched through his grandmother's papers until he found an
envelope bearing his father's name and regiment. There was no
letter inside to provide further clues. 'I wrote to St Louis asking
for my father's current address. I swallowed what they told me
[which was that they could not break the Invasion of Privacy
law]. I thought that I would never find him or see him, even
though I dreamed I would.'

His grandmother's deception left Howard too distressed to
stay with her so he went to live with his mother who had
by now married. Whilst he got on with her husband, he did
not feel settled. One can see that, regardless of his hostility,
Grandma as 'Mum' still represented 'home'. It was too late to
see his mother in that light or feel at ease living there. He turned
to an uncle who had represented the father-figure of his youth.
The man was now married and had a place of his own which
Howard had visited during school holidays. He was invited to
move in permanently.

This was to be a short-lived period of happiness; his uncle was
killed in a farming accident. Howard transferred his deep hunger
for a male figure of authority to a resumption of the search for his
father. He started by searching through a series of US telephone
books, a daunting task bearing in mind that every small town
in the US has its own directory. He also decided to try the St
Louis office again: 'I was determined this time and wrote several
letters. Each time I was told the man did not exist or that his
records were destroyed in a fire.'

Like many applicants who received this information from the

St Louis office, he was convinced that this was a stall to prevent him getting any further. However, later in this book there will be an eye-witness account of the size and ferocity of the fire.

Howard then saw a documentary on Central television called *Bloodline*, the idea for which had been suggested to them by a member of TRACE. The enquiries that followed the transmission were passed to the membership secretary.

'I think when I learned about TRACE it gave me the encouragement I needed, but most of all it put me in touch with people in the same situation. It is nice to talk to people in the same boat – they understand. Also, you do not have to feel embarrassed. I got all sorts of support from my family but my wife was the one who pushed me when I felt low, also my daughters.

'I wrote fourteen letters to the addresses from the phone books. One of them hit my brother and the other one went to my father. My brother went round to his mum's house and told her someone in England was trying to contact his dad. So, they phoned me. I did not tell them who I was but got the impression they had some idea.

'What made me go for Colorado where he came from was that that's where he retired. I got that from St Louis by asking for all releasable information on my father under the Freedom of Information Act.

'I came home from work, my wife was on the phone. She said, "You'd better sit down." I thought someone had died in the family. She said, "Someone in America wants to talk to you," and it turned out to be my father's wife. I asked a few questions to be sure I was talking to the right person. She told me to phone back the next day because of the time difference, but I couldn't wait. My wife and I stayed up till 1.30 a.m. until he came home from work.

'Waiting to phone was very nerve-racking. It was strange. I asked him a few questions. He just answered; never did ask me how or why. This gave me the impression that he had some idea who I was when I told him. (He hadn't known my mother was pregnant.) I asked how he felt about that and he said he wished he'd known sooner. When I asked how his wife would feel about me, he said he didn't know until he told her. I asked if he had any other children and he told me there was a girl and boy.'

Howard's father agreed that he could write to him and photographs were sent with the letter. There was no reply from America.

'That first phone call left me unsure of how I stood with him. Finding my father has changed me, so people say.

'After about two weeks, my wife gave my father a ring, without me knowing, to explain how I was feeling and that I would sooner know if he was going to acknowledge me. She said he was very nice on the phone, also that he would write to me, that it had been a big shock when I told him who I was.

'She asked if he had told his wife and he said he did not have any secrets from her and she would go along with whatever he decided. She also asked what his other children thought about having a brother in England. He said they were very pleased and wished they had known me when I was younger. She also questioned if there was any resemblance (by now they had received the photographs). He said there was and he liked the ones of my family.

'After all that, still no letter or call. The suspense is tearing me inside out but that is something you have to learn to live with. All the same, I'm glad I've found my dad. It gave me a great feeling, peace of mind, knowing I have a father, not just an image, even if he is out of reach. If I go no further than that, I've got past my wildest dreams, just talking to my dad. It may sound silly but that is how I feel. If things don't work out between me and my father I do not regret one minute of my time in finding him. It was one of the most important things in my life. I had to do it. I also think that when you find your father, you must give him room – time to adjust – even if it means hurting yourself with suspense.'

31

Sadly, Howard's patience has not paid off, no letters ever came and now he has discovered his father has changed his telephone number and is 'unlisted' – ex-directory.

Children soon learn the parameters beyond which their curiosity cannot be voiced. One who had discovered a hidden Bible with an American's name and address written inside had to learn its significance from half-whispered comments from careless friends of the family. This enabled her to deduce that she had been adopted by her grandmother because her mother, though engaged when the GI left, would not go to the States to marry him. Nor will she now give the child of this relationship enough information for him to be found. The secrecy has extended into the next generation. Her mother is now married and her other children think that their older sister is their aunt.

Diane W. of Weymouth dealt with a similar problem differently. She had known since she was eleven that her 'uncle' was really her grandfather: 'I didn't want to cause trouble between my grandparents for something that couldn't be changed, so I never asked questions.'

There could be no satisfactory answers by the time the truth was revealed to her at the age of thirty. Her mother had died when she was nineteen. The only hope was to find some of her friends who might be able to fill in the details of her romance with the GI. Diane placed an ad in the local paper. Frustratingly, there was no response. Then, by good fortune, she met someone who had nursed her mother before she died and had received her confidences. From this lady, Diane learned her father's name, that he had been stationed at Pit House, Chudleigh, Devon, prior to D-Day and that he was an ambulance driver.

This suggests that the reason he did not return for her mother was because he had become a casualty. Unfortunately, he does not have an unusual enough name to spring from any such lists without the necessary service number. This brings the search to a halt.

Steve F. in Essex also had a poor start. His mother died when he was three. Until then his father had been sending maintenance payments. Why they stopped has never been successfully explained. Perhaps it was because they came to his mother's name and no one knew how to have it changed.

But it is also possible that the grandparents feared that if the GI knew that the mother had died he might have come over to claim the child. For this reason they may not even have attempted to obtain further financial help from him.

When Steve was thirteen, his grandparents died. For a while he lived with his uncle but disputes arose and ill feeling caused him to take off. This prevented him from learning that the uncle had stayed in contact with his father until 1989.

After some delay, the GI phoned the council office in the area where he had been stationed to see if he could contact his son. Impatient with the slow response, he cut the conversation short, leaving the clerk there with an insufficient address. Fortunately, she felt this was too important an enquiry to ignore. On her own initiative, she traced Steve and passed on what little she had gleaned from the call from Texas.

Given the size of the state and the fact that his father's last name was Smith, it could have been a gargantuan task. The one useful clue was the name of the road and the fact that his father had said he lived on a trailer site. With the help of the police in that area, Steve was able to contact the owner of the campsite. He learned that his father was temporarily out of town, destination unknown. There was to be a nail-biting wait until he returned.

Steve's father was delighted to be found and promised to write. But he has proved to be unreliable; like too many GIs who suffered the war, he is now addicted to the bottle. Steve's one consolation was to learn that he has a sister and they have begun to write to each other so he now no longer feels alone.

Some people who suspect all is not as it should be do not voice their suspicions until adulthood. David B. of Nottingham was one of them. Perhaps he held back because he knew it would involve a confrontation with his adoptive mother who was his natural mother's cousin. His natural mother had married afterwards but although she had told her husband that she had an illegitimate child and had put it up for adoption, she fabricated the actual details of what happened, eliminating the fact that the father had been a GI.

'I decided at the age of forty-one that it was time I found out. I learned I had been conceived during the time that she had met an American soldier on a five-day pass. She cannot be exact on any other details, is not sure of the spelling of his last name but has said it was probably of Russian origin. She has positively eliminated what could have been a useful lead, given Nottingham was full of paratroopers. He was not one of them. There is only one tiny extra clue. He had a 'Jr' attached to his name.'

David realises this will be very little help since it was quite a common appellation among the American servicemen in the UK at that time.

David's adoptive mother had seen the danger of staying within his natural mother's orbit when he was young and had moved away. Sandra P. was also adopted by her natural mother's cousin, who was prepared to take a chance that there would be no interference: 'My natural mother was seen frequently and known as a family friend. We used to visit her over the years and take presents for her children.' [By now she had married.]

When Sandra was a teenager, her holiday plans fell through and her parents suggested she might like to stay with 'Aunty' who lived at a coastal resort.

'As with all holidays, you tend to say it would be nice to live there – which of course I did as a teenager. But now I feel this was naïve of me. I paid money for my keep and also baby-sat for her three children which at the time I never minded or objected to. It was when I returned home that the trouble started. My real mother tried to get me back through courts and solicitors – as an extra wage earner, I think, because I was then working in a bank, and also as a baby-sitter. This was when my parents told me all about the adoption because although they had told me previously it had not sunk in.

'The worry this gave my adoptive father caused him to be hospitalised for three months. I have never forgiven my real mother for that, rightly or wrongly. She came to the bank where I worked and created a scene which, as you can imagine, was very embarrassing and humiliating for a sixteen year old.

'At the court and with the solicitors, I stood up and said words to the effect that if she didn't want me when I needed her as a baby, I certainly didn't want or need her now, much to the joy of my adoptive parents. They were the best anyone could have. They were, have been and always will be my mum and dad, no matter what happens, even if I am lucky enough to find my GI father.

'I do feel my real mother missed out on a lot through greed or something else. I do not know why she could not have let things go on as they had done for sixteen years. She would have still seen me grow up, marry and have a family, for until then she was a family friend and as such was included in various get togethers, weddings, christenings, etc. But, because of the trouble caused around 1960, I wanted nothing more to do with her and instructed a solicitor to tell her so.'

All this ill feeling has hampered Sandra's search for her father. She has too few details and too common a name to get her very far. All she knows is that he was in the US Navy and came into Dartmouth during the build-up to the invasion of France. The most important item missing yet again is the service number.

Some of the GIs, realising that marriage to the girlfriend was too high a price to pay, did offer the cost of an abortion. If refused, the girl was on her own, unless she had sympathetic parents.

Michelle S. of Hertfordshire knows that her mother turned down this suggestion. She also knows that after she was born, her father wanted to see her but, understandably, this was not allowed. She has the sense to recognise the pressures attached to the circumstances of her birth and has not harboured any resentment against her father. There seemed no way of finding him to explain this until her mother received a letter from some old friends informing her that there was to be a reunion of the 'gang' who had hung out at the American base in the UK – would she come?

Michelle's father did not attend, but his address was on the roster. Her mother brought it back for her. It was at this stage that, hesitant to make direct contact, she approached me to be the intermediary.

My letter gave him a picture of his daughter, her hobbies and lifestyle. There is always the hope that something will match when they read this. I suggested he could either contact her through me or direct by telephone. What neither Michelle nor I realised was that we were presenting him with a dilemma. He was now a married man with two adopted children. She was his only natural child.

She was invited over to meet them but because her father made such a grudging acceptance of her she felt it was more like a rejection and has returned disappointed but much more appreciative of the family life her grandparents gave her.

Hugh D. now lives in Devon but he grew up in Stevenage, a town which drew in the GIs from the American base at Nuthampstead: 'I lived with my mother, her two sisters and my grandparents. My grandmother was always terrified that my father was going to turn up and snatch me.' This may be why they were all reticent about the GI's whereabouts as Hugh began to question them. In many cases, mothers in particular would not reveal all the details of their relationship because they were still protective of the GI who was *the* love of their life. 'I'm sure she is still in love with him. I'm positive she knows more than she's telling.'

Hugh's mother was an 'older' woman of thirty-four when she was romanced by her GI. Though a generation back from the majority of females flocking round the GIs, as an unmarried lady she would have been just as innocent. Born in 1910, she was a social victim of World War I, suffering from the decimation of men who would have been potential husbands when she reached marriageable age. One can see how the GIs brought a flutter of excitement to such reluctant spinsters.

Hugh's upbringing became a family affair:

'My mother went out to work and I was more or less looked after by all of them. I knew my father was a GI from the moment I could understand and the only time it bothered me was one Christmas. The whole family was together – aunts, uncles, cousins. We were all sitting round the table and I started crying. "How come they've all got fathers – where's mine?" One of my uncles came round to comfort me and it was over within an hour.'

As Hugh grew up he wanted to know more about his father. He is very scared he is running out of time because, like his mother, his father was older then the average GI who was in the UK. His research has taken him as far as the town of Baltimore but he is fearful to take that final step which could cause an old man too much of a shock. Meanwhile, he has compiled a detailed file on the now deserted base where his parents met and has a collection of photographs taken from every possible angle.

However tightly a secret is held in a family, it should never be considered safe from discovery. An example of this occurred in 1990 after I sent to America a copy of a *Sunday Express* article which related to members of TRACE who needed to know the medical history of their American families. The recipient recognised in one case history the name of a town where a friend, now in Ohio, had met and married a GI. With the hope that this person might provide some useful clues to a missing GI father mentioned in the article, it was sent on. In the end, this article was to provide the answer to a forty-year-old village mystery. The friend identified this man looking for his father as the son of the sister of a school friend who had faded out of sight at that time.

THREE

Some of the Cuckoos
Stayed in the Nest

It is known that there were some couples who agreed to a 'no
questions asked' pact of separate lives until the war was over.
However, this amicable arrangement could flounder if proof of
a wife's infidelity emerged in the shape of a baby.

Sometimes, though, their married status gave women a con-
venient cover. Pregnancy was perfectly acceptable if a finger
count against the date the husband had been with her could
be justified. One wife, under threat from her parents not to
leave her husband for a GI, was saved by a 'premature' baby
which tied in with the time of his return. The child was raised in
total ignorance until the mother's death. She then discovered that
loyalty to her wartime lover had impelled her mother to leave a
letter and photographs. By doing this, the woman destroyed her
daughter's sense of identity.

Dates that could not be accounted for and already existing children
within the marriage meant that not all these liaisons could have
such a simple solution.

Susan R. from Shropshire was to be put up for adoption rather
than endanger her mother's marriage, but her mother found that
she couldn't go through with the plan. Her sister offered to take
in the baby and it was there that the GI came to see her:

'He held me in his arms and my mother gave him a letter and
a photograph. She has told me that he had wanted to go and see
her husband and tell him about me but by then she had decided

38

to stay with the marriage. [Her tie may well have been the son she already had.] For the first few years I stayed with my aunt, visiting my mother only when her husband was away.'

What can now be seen as a cold-blooded and confusing arrangement for the child was probably viewed by the sisters as in everyone's best interest. However, when Susan was four, she was taken back by her mother. It is not clear what prompted this decision, but because her mother had by now had another child with her husband and some years had elapsed, perhaps she felt that her marriage had stabilised.

'I went to live with them. I never noticed anything at first because I was too young, but as time went on I would hear Dad shout at my mum, "Go back to your Yank." I didn't know what he meant but he used to say it all the time. I also noticed that he never sat by me or put his arm round me like he did with my sister, but I put it down to her being the youngest. When I look back, I think my mum was too afraid to show me much affection when he was about. Anyhow, the rows got worse as I got older and one night something was said and I thought, one of us doesn't belong to Dad, but I really didn't think it was me. Then one night I came home from school soaking wet and went upstairs to change, came down, and Dad asked me to go out and post his football coupon. I protested that I had just changed and it was still pouring with rain. Well, he went mad. Mum said she would go but he said to her in front of me, "I don't want you or your lot to do anything for me." I knew then that all the rows, everything, it was me who didn't belong to him. He went out to post his coupon and I said to my mother, "Don't I belong to Dad?" and she said, "You might as well know now, you don't."

'Dad never said another word about it again. Mum told him I knew. I think it was a relief for him. I don't think we ever looked each other in the eye again. We spoke to each other but there was never anything there after that. I was upset for a long time. I was embarrassed to ask my mother anything. She did tell me things over the years – that my father was

American and from Missouri, he was thirty-three, had blond hair, green eyes, and was six foot tall.'

This was the picture of her father Susan carried in her mind for a long time. She wanted to find him but didn't know how to start. 'I couldn't ask Mum to help me so I just went on with my life. When I got married and had my daughters I never thought about it too much, I was too busy. Then I started thinking he might get in touch with me, but he never did.'

Susan is not the only one to voice that feeling or wonder why her father, if he knew about her, didn't try to search. But of course if he had had an affair with a married woman, he would have felt it best not to intrude again.

Susan had to wait until her mother's husband died before she could question her freely. She realised that the subject of her birth was very sensitive: 'I think she really loved him; in fact I think she still does. I hope he loved her and thought about her once in a while.'

It was through seeing my appearance on BBC's *Daytime Live* when I was discussing TRACE that Susan eventually discovered what happened to her father. Because she knew that he had lived in the same state as Harold Ludwig, a 'friend' of TRACE, it was suggested that she send him the details. He was able to find some people in a telephone book who turned out to be relatives: 'The sad thing is that my father never married or had any other family. If only I could have found him earlier.' At least she now has photographs of her father and some of the gaps have been filled in. She is saddened that he went through a lonely life without knowing more about her. His family have welcomed her and there are frequent letters and telephone calls. A visit is planned. She has found that 'unless you have been in this situation, no one knows how you feel. Even my husband and daughters don't. As close as I am to them, they can't understand what it means to me to have traced my father.'

Someone whose circumstances started similarly to Susan's, but who had fewer clues, is the result of a British soldier taking home a GI he met in a pub to meet his wife.

'When he returned six months after I was born, he threatened to leave her if she didn't get rid of me. She already had four other children – what could she do? I was put in a children's home. She is now most reluctant to discuss my real father except to say that he promised to keep in touch and she never heard from him again.'

This domestic drama took place in an area where the US troops were training for the invasion of France, so it is possible that this GI did not survive. His daughter's search for him is hampered by the fact that she does not know his full name: 'I am told that everyone called him "Rooster". His last name is quite a common one. I thought if I tried an ad in the *Army Times* someone might come forward who could tell me something. No one did.'

Some couples' attempt at reconciliation didn't always work. Patricia D. from Hertfordshire did not know that the man her mother divorced when she was two was not her real father.

'When my mother married again, my stepfather wanted me to change my surname. I refused and it must have upset him. [She was all of six at the time.] He was very good to me but I could never call him "Dad" to his face although I always referred to him that way to my friends.'

Still believing the man who had divorced her mother to be her real father, Patricia's loyalties stayed with him and she did not understand why he never came to see her.

'Then, when I was sixteen, my cousin came to stay. She found my mother's divorce papers in the attic. The reason for it was adultery and the correspondent was named as Ancil Bowling. My name was mentioned as not being the child of the marriage. I was very upset at not being told by my mother. My cousin also found letters and pictures which is how I found out I was half American, which really pleased me. I also learned I had a half-sister called Paulette.'

One can picture the relish with which this teenage visitor related the details of the family 'scandal' as the papers came to light.

41

They also disclosed that the GI had been wounded in France and was likely to be dead. It was some years before Patricia confronted her mother with the information and was told she was not completely sure that the man had died. This opened up the possibility of searching for him, but Patricia did not know how to start because her mother professed to not being able to remember his address.

In 1981 she wrote to the US Embassy. They referred her to the National Personnel Records Center in St Louis which was their usual procedure then. But without a service number they could not help her either.

> 'Then, in 1986, I saw a programme on Central TV called *Bloodline*. I realised that there were a lot of people trying to find fathers. My enquiry was sent to TRACE who gave me a lot of encouragement and useful addresses. I found out that my father had survived the war and remember feeling overjoyed about it. As he had been wounded, I wrote to the Veterans' Administration office to see if he had claimed a benefit.'

The most successful of these searches are conducted by people who use their initiative. In Patricia's case it led to an unwanted discovery. 'They wrote to say they were sorry to inform me that he had died in 1980 in Tennessee. I was heartbroken, but felt the need to at least find the half-sister my mother had told me about.'

By applying for her father's death certificate, she thought she would be able to see who was next of kin but the authorities would not hand it over without proof that she was a relative.

Refusing to give up, Patricia visited the Holborn Reference Library in London to search through the telephone books of towns in Tennessee. There are people who do not have the advantage of more than their father's name who have gone there to comb through town after town in every state in the hope of finding him.

Patricia began a list of everyone with the same last name as her father: 'I wrote to several saying that I was a relation of the late Ancil Bowling and wanted any information they could give me on the family. One of the letters reached Helen, my step-mother. She thought I was doing a family tree and sent some details.' Within a few days, this lady realised who Patricia really was and wrote a less formal letter: 'Your father told me soon after he came home that he could have a child over there.' What followed was a wonderful, kind, long letter about him, filling in the years after her father had returned to the US. She also said she had told her children about their English half-sister and they were all delighted.

'I don't know how you feel about me, but I loved your father with all my heart and I will love you as I do my own. I know that this is what he would have wanted. I will never get to England but if you can get over here, I would love to have you and I know the kids would love to see you.'

Joyfully, Patricia made plans to go to Tennessee. Waiting for her were four half-sisters, three half-brothers and their respective partners. 'We got on so well together it seemed like I had known them all my life. They were so welcoming and excited about finding me. They told me many stories about my "daddy".' This, of course, is the most important part of these Anglo-American meetings – learning about the father.

Patricia finally had her identity; everywhere she went she was introduced as 'Ancil's daughter'. As such, she was included in a big family reunion of eighty relatives.

This story concludes by illustrating one of the kinds of different worlds that British children may find themselves stepping into when they visit their American families. Not all reunions are as pleasing as Patricia's was to her. She had entered the Bible Belt – full of church-going communities. All their get togethers invariably have religious overtones. 'We had a wonderful time singing gospel songs with my brothers playing their guitars.' In Patricia's case, although she didn't have a religious upbringing in the UK, she couldn't help but be swept away by the spirit of such occasions.

There is another important reason why some couples attempted a reconciliation. This was when wives who had been led to believe that their British husband was 'missing believed killed' had to readjust to the fact that he was alive after all. One such 'widow' with two sons had repaired her life to the extent that she had accepted a proposal of marriage from the GI who had fathered her daughter. However, when she received word that her husband was not dead but held as a prisoner of war, she ended the romance. The child of that liaison became the only girl in a family of many boys. All she has as a clue to her real father is that she was given the name of her paternal grandmother.

Another tangled marriage involved a GI, but he was not the cause of its breakup. The woman's husband had already left her for someone else but he used her pregnancy as an excuse to get custody of their son. This left the mother very bitter and unable to talk to her daughter about the circumstances of her birth.

'I was the immaculate conception,' says Rosemary J. of Devon. The rest of the family maintained the conspiracy of silence. Led by the mother, the attitude was 'we don't talk about this', but as Rosemary says, 'A child is a person with feelings and it too deserves status and respect for the person it is, not the way it was born. My mother spent forty-two years hiding behind the truth and if I ever mentioned my father she went cold.'

Her mother finally managed to tell her his home state and a garbled version of his last name which indicated he was of Polish extraction. Perusing telephone books of towns in that area led to a name which resembled her father's enough to be worth a letter. It was carefully worded so as not to make any assumptions which would intrude on his family life.

There was such a long interval afterwards that Rosemary assumed she had made a mistake. Then, her telephone rang with a call from a US base in England. It was her half-brother who was doing a tour of duty there. His father had written to tell him about a newly-found sister and he was determined to be the first to meet her. Through him she learned about the rest of her family which included the fact that her father had married when he returned home from the war. It was not long before she went to meet all of them:

'It was a trip of a lifetime. I can honestly tell you we now have the great feeling of being part of a family. We all got on very well and found we had many things in common. My father is quite a character and has a wonderful sense of humour which made

44

my thirteen-year-old son laugh a great deal. He made sure we learned some Polish words and enjoyed their traditional food along with the American diet. Saying goodbye was tough for us all and even my six foot Dad was wiping away a tear and saying a Polish blessing to his newly-found grandson. I've come home with a good feeling – what more can I ask? I have actually stopped wondering who my father is.'

Unfortunately, her mother has proved hostile to what happened but one has to understand her feelings too. In such circumstances, mothers are bound to feel a little jealous or perhaps fear that they will lose this child to the excitement of that American reunion with the father.

Some of the marriages damaged by a wife's affair with a GI had been interrupted at an early stage by the British husband's departure for war. Whether one condones this or not, their hunger for the attention of a man was understandable. There might have seemed to be some safety in numbers when agreeing to make up a foursome with a single sister and two GIs. It didn't work out that way for Norma C.'s mother who lived in London.

Her husband had been serving abroad for two years and the scenario of a lonely, vulnerable wife was neatly in place. There was a child of the marriage so she was forgiven her indiscretion when the husband returned, but he could not forget.

'Life at home was always stormy; it seemed to be about me. I felt different and could never understand what was wrong with me. I always tried to be a good daughter, but nothing pleased him. Mum and "Dad" used to stop speaking to each other for weeks on end. Now I realise why. I feel angry and should have been told the truth. Everyone knew my business except for me.'

Norma understands that her mother must have been in a desperate situation when she was born. She had tried to be honest and had written to ask her husband for a divorce. It was as difficult for him; he had been away from home a long time and had yet to see the child of their marriage. 'For the rest of her life, she tried to make it up to her husband but he never forgave her.

'I was first told about "Larry" when I was seven or eight but not that he was my father.' One can see that this poor woman was dying to talk about this romance. 'Larry' had said he would wait for her. 'There was a picture of a GI in the house, then it disappeared. My mother gave me a brass cross when I was small saying it belonged to an American soldier. I have always kept it.'

In her teens Norma did try to find out who was really her father but by now her mother deflected any leading questions.

'Things were made far worse when their daughter died at the age of seven. I felt sad for them; I felt sad that it was not me. I know he would have preferred it. He has said it. He ruined so many important occasions. On my wedding day, he never spoke to me or to anyone else for that matter. Mum said he didn't want me to go. I don't believe that.'

When Norma talked over her situation with her mother's sisters they suggested that 'Larry' might be her father.

'Several things that had been said over the years now began to fall into place. I decided I would write to Mum [who now lived some distance away]. The response was an angry phone call denying that 'Larry' was my father. I knew she was lying. It hurt. I loved her very much. I felt that if I didn't find out the truth, I would go mad. I talked it through with a social worker who suggested I contact the American Embassy to see if they had anyone who could help.

'So my friendship with Pamela, Sophia and TRACE began. I have written many letters, usually one a week. I was put in touch with Harold Ludwig ['friend' of TRACE] who has made many phone calls on my behalf.'

The reason for this was because Harold lives in a neighbouring state to Kansas which Norma thought was her father's home state. The aunt who had been part of the other couple in that fateful foursome had married her GI and now lived in the States. She had been reluctant to help while her husband was alive, but had finally furnished Norma with his wartime address book which listed a 'Lawrence' who they were guessing was the right person. Her mother argued this was incorrect but would not produce an alternative.

With so few clues Norma's efforts have so far been in vain. There was great excitement when she found someone with a matching name in Kansas but he turned out to be a veteran of the Korean war. She has since tracked one down in Georgia. His telephone number is 'unlisted'. Harold Ludwig wrote a letter as an intermediary but it was ignored, as was a plea from Norma to at least confirm or deny he is the person she is trying to reach.

The answer finally came after Norma wrote to a social worker at the County Hall in Savannah. A woman from the Adult Protective Service went to investigate and wrote to tell Norma that this Mr McCloud was black and had never left the US.

'There are times when I've wanted to give up but something makes me carry on. If I do not continue, I know I will regret it for the rest of my life.' Her mother is now dead and she keeps her search from her stepfather because 'there has been enough pain'.

If the child was absorbed into the family, it doesn't alter the sense of shock or betrayal. Several men accepted the baby they found when they came back as their 'fortunes of war' and did not allow this to damage their relationship with the child.

Until early 1990, Lorraine E. of Worcestershire thought that she was a member of a close-knit group with two older brothers and one younger. Then, one of those brothers inadvertently shook the family tree. With that, their mother's deeply hidden secret fell out.

Lorraine was asked to gather up her family birth certificates for the project he proposed and realised hers was a short form – different from the others:

'The following day I phoned the registrar and asked about obtaining a full birth certificate. She checked the records and explained that the possible reason for my short form copy was due to the fact that there was no mention of my father on the original. Even at this point I was totally naïve. I enquired why this should be and she coldly told me that I was probably illegitimate.'

We must assume that this clerk in the office was of a younger generation who would have seen no importance in such a bald statement. She probably had no idea she was sending her caller into a state of shock.

'I am forty-five years old. I cannot truly describe my feelings at that moment – stunned seems inadequate. I just remained sitting by the phone. I couldn't really believe what I had just heard. Within days I received a copy of my full birth certificate and this seemed only to deepen my hurt – a printed confirmation of my fears. I found it necessary to escape for hours in the car – all direction and meaning seemed to have vanished. I felt hopelessly alone with an immense, impossible task of finding the truth.'

Lorraine turned first to her vicar who was helpful and checked baptism and church records. This only confirmed her suspicions that the man she had always thought of as her father was not.

What parents do not seem to consider when they hide such information to 'protect' the child is how it will decimate them as adults. Suddenly they have become a person they do not know.

Through the vicar, Lorraine was able to contact her godmother who had assumed until then that she was aware of her natural father.

'He turned out to be a medical officer based in Malvern during the war but my godmother could not remember his name. She did remember a lot about the man she had dated who was his best friend, in fact offered me photographs of him – she felt I needed something belonging to my real father and it was the best she could do.

'I was deeply hurt and confused. I felt bitter towards my mother's lack of responsibility. She should have told me. I had the ultimate right to know. The incident doesn't bother me. My mother had a perfect right to her privacy but I too have the right to know my parentage. I felt envious of 'normal' people. I no longer knew who I was. My family were no longer my real relations, all that I had ever known had vanished. I also suffered a terrible sense of guilt – having this knowledge which I was obviously not meant to hold.'

In spite of feeling that everything she had known as real seemed no longer to be true, habit made her still think of both parents as hers. Since they were elderly and in poor health, it seemed wrong to ask questions. 'I feared what the shock might do to them so I talked to my brothers. The eldest began to remember terrible rows and going to court; also being warned, "If you want to keep your sister, you must be good." ' One can assume from this that her mother's husband adopted Lorraine. 'He certainly wasn't here when I was conceived because he fought in the Battle of Anzio that year.'

Fortunately, she had a supportive set of siblings with whom she could discuss what to do for the best: 'My brothers and I eventually decided that I had to approach my mother. Initially, I rang her and she instantly denied the facts.' It was not until Lorraine told her mother that she had her adoption certificate that she very unwillingly agreed to talk to her.

'Her attitude was very selfish. She was horrified that I had spoken to my brothers, also my husband and children. She accused me of going behind her back. She was more distressed over her own appearance than aware of the terrible hurt it had caused me. She did not offer me any information but blamed me for opening up a forty-five-year-old secret.'

It was only after her brother phoned their mother and warned her that they would start to question the neighbours for clues that she was more forthcoming with a name and address. 'I am determined to find the truth. I need to know my true identity. I cannot go on with my life when I don't know who I really am. Perhaps it is too late.'

This proved to be the case because the US Embassy advised Lorraine to contact TRACE who had a 'friend' in the area. First it was discovered that there was a missing letter in her father's name which proved he was dead.

Lorraine has now made her first ever flight to the States to meet her nephew and niece. Through them she learned something of her father's background, met some of his friends, visited his old school and saw where he worked. All of which was captured on video. 'I've come home with my family history on tape.'

Sheila C. from Salisbury made her discovery at a younger age:

'I had a very good relationship with my "dad", then when I was twelve years old and bored, a thunderstorm prevented any outdoor activity so I decided to tidy out the sideboard. In a special tin, in which my mother kept all important papers, there was an unmarked, sealed envelope. I'd seen it many times before and I just knew it contained the secret of my two surnames. Over the years, I had asked why I had a different one for the doctor and hospital. Always my question was brushed aside and the air would be heavy with embarrassment so I would never persist. I steamed open the envelope [Enid Blyton's Famous Five stories have much to answer for!] to reveal my birth certificate telling me that my father was a Joseph Harris, a 1st Sergeant in the US Army Air Force. I was fascinated – it seemed exciting and made me different.'

Such a discovery made during childhood is bound to add to its importance – children enjoy mystery; adults don't deal with it as easily when it involves themselves.

A little bit of deduction on Sheila's part led nowhere in particular because she had a brother who was four years older than her. To this child this had to mean nothing could be wrong:

'I wasn't exactly sophisticated. I couldn't really understand all the secrecy because obviously "Dad" must have known about the situation as Mum had been receiving American letters for most of my young life. I used to see them in her handbag but if I asked about them, I never received a real answer.'

At fourteen, Sheila was officially adopted by her father.

'And Mum was therefore forced to explain about my real father. (I did admit I already knew.) She showed me a picture of this handsome man and the birthday and Christmas cards he'd sent me right up till I'd been eight years old. I have to say, I felt rather cheated about that aspect of it all. My real father had cared but my mother had not seen fit to allow me that knowledge. Anyway, to a fourteen year old, it was so romantic, but I had no desire to find him then – what for? I had a loving father already. There'd been cuddles, tickles and teasing, in fact he treated me better than he did my brother – his own son.'

Eventually, Sheila realised that her mother wanted her to find her natural father. As an adult, Sheila admits she was not interested to know what traits of personality she might have inherited from her father and why he had deserted her mother and given up writing over the years.

Around that time she married and lived for a while in Australia. While there, she contacted the Salvation Army in Sydney to see if they could help. Subconsciously, she may have felt she was now far away enough from the 'dad' she loved so as not to hurt his feelings. 'The Salvation Army traced Joe through an elderly aunt and in 1969 I wrote him a long letter and sent photos informing him that he would soon have a grandson too.'

In cases like this where the GI was aware he had left a child in England, an approach usually receives an enthusiastic response. Sheila did not receive a reply.

'I never really knew whether the aunt actually passed on that letter. I certainly found it difficult to believe that it had been ignored. Later of course, I learned he had received it but still thought best to leave well alone and considering the circumstances of our lives [by now he was married] it was a wise decision.'

She then left the search for her father in abeyance until 1982. This time, knowing the area where he lived, she was able to contact the Salvation Army in Los Angeles. 'I heard nothing from them for a while, then came a very snotty letter from the

Salvation Army in London saying they did not undertake such investigations unless a marriage had taken place!'

There does seem to be a variance in how the Salvation Army respond, but in recent years their International Service have been sending enquiries they cannot handle to TRACE.

Quite unexpectedly, in February 1983, Sheila received a letter from her father. 'This started a satisfactory correspondence. We planned a visit for Christmas but my mother beat us to it. She left England to join him in September.' Sheila prefers not to enlarge on this. As she says, 'It's where mother and I agree to differ over the handling of this affair.' This is to do with her loyalty to the 'dad' who raised her and the fact her mother deserted him for the man who must have been the love of her life. Two years ago, she married her GI Joe.

'Now everyone's lives are sorted out and everything has worked out well for all concerned. People say that my father – Joe – is very lucky to have had a second chance but that's only because I persisted in my searches. For my part, I'm glad the mystery is solved; the facts are out in the open; the family skeleton has been laid to rest. I understand what makes me tick; I appreciate even more what England means to me and what my "dad" means to me. I also like having another side of my life in America; I still like feeling different. Finding one's real father does not necessarily mean a great surge of parental love on either side, just because you share the same blood. I feel that my father loves me more than I love him, but he's had no other daughter or son to love all these years whereas I have had a jolly good father.'

With this man who is her adoptive father, Sheila is in the fortunate position of enjoying the love of someone who did not blame her for the GI in her mother's life. Not every British male was or is that considerate.

FOUR

Stepfathers: Bad, Indifferent and Sometimes Good

Resentment and jealousy rankled in the British male's chest long after the last wartime GI had left the UK. Some conveniently chose to forget that they too had had a good time with the local girls in the countries where they had been stationed – indeed may have deflowered a few virgins! In the Britain of the 1940s where sexual equality was yet unknown, men saw it as their prerogative to expect a virgin bride. She might have had another explanation for the absence of this condition but it didn't work if there was a child.

Those who condescended to marry 'spoiled goods' could and did lay down conditions. It is almost unbelievable how many women were willing to put up with appalling treatment for the sake of the magic prefix 'Mrs' – more especially if she had already suffered from being an unmarried mother. These women accepted that the husband could dictate terms and that the child in most cases would have to be considered excess baggage.

The adjustment for the child could never be easy, especially if it had till then been raised in the safe, cosy environment of Mum and Grandma.

'I can remember being very unhappy when my mother took me to live with this strange man. He was very cold towards me and of course my mother was uncomfortable in showing me any affection if he was around. My mother had another child when I was nine, three years after the marriage. Of course Bert was very proud of her and I was pushed even further into

53

the background. I really resented her because she could do no wrong – she was a real spoiled brat – whereas I had to creep around because I did not want to draw attention to myself in case I was picked on. It was always a case of making so much of anything she achieved and nothing of anything I did.

'In the event I didn't make any effort because whatever I did was wrong and he took away all my confidence. I was happiest when he worked abroad and left Mum at home with us. She tried desperately to make things up to me but I had to promise not to tell him if she bought me any little presents.

'Sadly she died suddenly at the age of forty-two. About two months afterwards he came to see me and told me he had adopted me and that my real father had been a GI. He said that I was an embarrassment to him as he was only sixteen years older than me and while my mother was alive he had had to pass me off as his own. He said he did this to please my mother because she could not bring herself to tell me the truth. Of course I was devastated, I didn't even know who I was. I went straight round to my grandmother and questioned her about it. She was upset that my mother had gone to her grave without telling me and that he had taken it upon himself to spill the beans. I felt so upset for my poor mum – what she must have gone through.

'I have grown a lot closer to my half-sister since she has had a family and when we talk about our childhood she can remember me being picked on and it upsets her when I say that I would not like my childhood back again.

'The last conversation I had with my stepfather was on the phone when he told me he had made a new will. He said he was going to leave a certain amount to me but four times as much to my sister as she had three children. I was very hurt and it was then that I decided I did not want any more contact with him. He obviously could not cope with the fact that my mother had wanted me with her. I must have been a constant thorn in his side.

Her mother had left her an important legacy: the name and location of her American father. A name matching his was found in the town through International Directory Enquiries but that person denies he is the father. She has now written a letter of explanation and is waiting to see if he will reply.

Many women were forced by their husbands to destroy their mementoes of their GIs. Others were lost in various ways.

The mother of Dyane P. from Milton Keynes had been working as a milkmaid when she met her American boyfriend. They had a steady relationship which ended when he was killed in a plane crash. His CO sent her the GI's identity bracelet.

Her job came with accommodation on the farm but once she realised she was pregnant, she knew she was in danger of being thrown out by her employers. She managed to keep her condition a secret for eight months before being evicted. With both parents dead, she was homeless until a cousin agreed to take her in and look after the baby so she could go to work to support it. However, Dyane was so badly neglected it was reported by the neighbours.

In despair, the mother took off with the child, intent on ending it all by jumping into the path of a speeding train. She was stopped on the bridge by someone who became a Good Samaritan by finding a couple who would foster the baby while she worked. During that time, her purse containing letters from her lost love was stolen.

Dyane was happy with the couple she assumed were her parents.

> 'I was six and a half when my mum, who I thought was a nice aunty who came with presents, arrived to take me away. I was told I was leaving my "mum" and "dad" whom I really loved, to go and live with "Aunty Win" because she was my real mother and was getting married and wanted me to live with her and her new husband. Of course, I didn't want to go but had no choice. I had only met this man four times and was very afraid. I remember very well when my foster mum took me to what was to be my new home where we were going to live with my stepfather's family until they got a home of their own.'

There was an acute housing shortage after the war and it was quite common for newlyweds to live in with one or other set of parents.

Some care does seem to have been taken to make this transition comfortable for the child. Dyane was taken off for a walk by one of her stepfather's sisters who also lived in what was to be her new home; there were about seven in the house, all complete strangers to the child.

> 'My old mum talked to my new mum about me. It was awful living there; I was in the way. My mum was told by her in-laws that she should have left me where I was to give the marriage a chance but she said I had gone through enough and it was her place to look after me.'

This anxious mother did not realise that her misplaced loyalty was to cost her child dear. Dyane's stepfather took from her the only memento left of her GI father – the precious ID bracelet – saying, 'All good Yanks are dead ones and never forget it.' He was reported by the neighbours to the police for ill-treating the child and warned he would be in trouble if he did not cease. It made no difference, and the child found she dare not mention anything about her real father – not then nor during the years she was growing up. It is only in the last four years since this man has died that she has begun to find out anything about the GI but, 'My mother's memory seems to have blotted out everything after the upheaval she suffered so I know very little. There has been a lot of sadness in my life that I don't think would have occurred if only Louis James Pozlin had been around.' It would be a wonderful thing if someone recognised this name and could tell his daughter even the tiniest detail about her dead father. She has no idea where he came from in USA.

Frank H. who now lives in Kent had first shared the comfort of his grandmother's home while his mother went out to work. Then she married. For a while, everything stayed just as calm, if more crowded:

> 'Finally, we were assigned a council house in Rotherhithe – well it was really a Nissen hut – and that's when the real

trouble started. My stepfather was now in charge and could do as he liked. I wasn't his and every time he looked at me I was a reminder of what had happened before he met my mum. Every time he picked on me I ran back to my gran and once I said to her, "Why does he keep picking on me?" She said, "Because you're a Bloody Yank, son." I said, "What's a Yank?" "A Yank is a GI," she replied, and I just stood there, eleven years old and didn't know what to say. She said, "You're somebody else's, not his." She didn't like my stepfather anyway. I went back to my mum. "Gran says my dad's a Yank," and she said, "Take no bloody notice." '

There was no question of Frank calling his stepfather 'Dad'.

'I didn't call him anything, he was so horrible. I hated him; he was drinking heavily and never went out to work. He was a total layabout. Finally I coined the name "Soberless" which suited him beautifully. My mother ended up having seven children by him. What could she do but put up with him?

'My grandmother's house became my "bunkhole". She saved my sanity. Every time there was trouble, that's where I ran. I was lucky to have the intelligence to know this wasn't a normal life. Luckily I had the key to Gran's house.'

Even though Frank didn't know his real father's name, the fact that he knew he had an American father made it his most treasured possession.

'I'd daydream about him at school; sit in the classroom and be looking out of the window thinking all the time about my father, wondering where he was. I was obsesseed with it. Living in "Dirty Deptford", as it was called, I'd watch the glossy American movies: it was like never-never land.

'I'd think, I bet he drives a great big Cadillac, I bet he's clean and smart. Up there in my mind, I was bombarded with what could have been. Why didn't my mum marry him, why didn't my mum go back to America with him? I never discussed it with my mates. They knew nothing about him. It was private and my secret weapon. I didn't want to share it with anybody.

No one else could touch me because I knew something they didn't know.

'I used to sometimes play little games if I took out a girlfriend and we'd go and see an American film. We'd say it must be wonderful and I'd say, I bet you don't know what I know. I used it as protective armour and it definitely helped me get through the bad times, but I never discussed it with anybody.'

It took Frank another six years to get a hint of his father's name:

'We were down at Gran's. There was this horse-race on TV. All of a sudden, my mum said, "That's your father's name." The horse was called Owen Antony. I was so dumbfounded I never asked her any more and she was off out of the door to go shopping with my gran. I never got any further either except to learn she was only sixteen when she met the GI and he had a sun-tan.'

On this flimsy evidence, Frank decided his father must have come from either Florida or California. He has visited both places, combing telephone books, going on radio, making pleas for help. His last visit to Florida was on a do-or-die basis. He sold his flourishing business and started one there to support the family while he made an intensive search for his father. 'I thought if I was there it would be better. There'd never been enough time when I was on holiday.' With so little in the way of clues, he began to realise he was working on an impossible task. He also began to worry about his teenage daughter.

'I went to collect her from school one day and the place was humming with police. I asked if they were having a special visiting day like they sometimes do in British schools and found out it was always like that. I thought then, this wasn't for us.'

Frank is now back in England to stay, has bought another home and started a new business. This willingness to begin again could hark back to American pioneer ancestors. However, he has come to terms with the fact that it is now very unlikely he will ever find his father and is doubtful that he even has the correct name. 'Owen' was not very common then; his mother could well have misheard. There is a possibility it may be 'Olin' which is much more American but would have been unknown in England then. It could equally follow that he could have an incorrect last name. His mother, now widowed, still refuses to remember anything more about the time when as a young, impressionable girl she was overwhelmed by a 'flashy, sun-tanned Yank'.

'David' was such a popular boy's name in the 1940s, that several of them thread through this book.

David C. of Glamorgan, like Frank, lived with his grandmother and mother for a while then, like Dyane who was mentioned earlier, moved in with his stepfather's family. He did not realise that the cruelty his stepgrandmother exhibited towards him was due to the dislike she shared with her son when it came to 'Yanks'.

David's unhappiness increased when they eventually moved into a place of their own and his mother had more children. His stepfather treated them totally differently from him. When the situation became too oppressive, he would make a run for his grandmother's house. She protested to her daughter on behalf of the boy but it didn't help.

From the age of fifteen, David had been aware of looks and innuendos in the street and local shops:

'I began to feel that people were talking about me, and as it happens they were. It was a great, gossipy, working-class area. I began to be pretty upset. Then, one Friday night, my stepfather laid into me. He had a terribly vicious tongue. I was devastated. My mother stood back and said nothing.

'I fled the house, walked the five miles to my grandmother and was in floods of tears. She confused me by apologising. "I'm sorry, if it hadn't been for me, perhaps you wouldn't be in this position now, but your mother was so young that I didn't want her to go to America. Perhaps I should have let her."

'I was taken totally by surprise. She went on to explain that my father was an American in the Navy, his name was John James Brown. He came to ask Grandma's permission to marry my mother. She said he was very nice but he was very young. At the time, I was so upset, I never asked any further questions.

'Nothing more was said until somebody near where I lived began to make jibes at me and I thought, for God's sake, what is going on, why are they keeping on at me? And I remember going into the house pretty upset and saying, "Everybody's talking about me," and going to my room. My stepfather came up and actually showed some compassion when he said, "We should have told you everything before now." My mother never followed up with anything else.'

David left school at sixteen, and hated the job he went into so he joined the Navy. He admits there was a fleeting hope that this might get him to America though he had no further clues by which he might have looked for his father.

When he came out of the Navy he developed a business which ended up employing several hundred people.

'But still in my adult life, in this part of the world, I had people talking about me. Then, in a dinner party conversation with friends of the family, I began to learn something of the circumstances of my birth, of how my parents met – two sisters and two sailors making up a foursome. I was forty when this piece of news came to me and I thought, why at my age and time of life is it so important to people?'

Children of GIs do not always realise that for the young women of their mothers' era it was the most exciting time of their lives – an event of local history to be relished into the present day.

His mother was still proving reticent but finally David's wife managed to extract from her the fact that the American had been fair, blond and very quiet. This was intriguing because it was a description that matched their son. They were unable to take the questioning any further so again he put the problem aside.

It was not until David was diagnosed as having a medical

condition that could render him immobile in a few years that questions were raised about his paternal medical history in case there was a hereditary factor. There was now some urgency in finding the father but all he had was the name John James Brown. This had been grudgingly confirmed by his mother with only one other fact: that he came from Nashville, Tennessee.

David made telephone calls to official bodies in the States and enlisted professional help from investigators but nothing came up on the whereabouts of a John James Brown.

'I decided that since my aunt had been part of this foursome she might be able to help. She told me they had met the sailors in London and gone back to Plymouth where they were based and stayed in a flat with them. She said my father's name was not John James Brown but agreed he did come from Nashville, Tennessee.

'It seemed that the best thing to do would be to go to America and so we flew to Tennessee. There I found a very helpful lady in the Nashville Veterans' Administration office but, using my father's name, she got nothing out of her computer. The alternative was to ask her if she could find a record of my aunt's boyfriend and out came his name and an address in New Mexico, and my wife and I chased off down there to see him.'

The man was delighted to reminisce about his wartime affair in England but could only remember David's father as being called 'Cookie' because he worked in the mess aboard ship. Their landing craft had gone down in the invasion but he couldn't remember if 'Cookie' had gone aboard a second craft.

'We were pretty dispirited when we returned to Nashville to get the flight back. There was just time to phone the lady in the Veterans' office to tell her what had happened. Then I thought to give her the name my aunt told me was my father's even though my mother insisted to the last it was John James Brown.

'We were actually in the hotel foyer waiting for our taxi to the airport when the VA lady came on the phone to say she had not only found the name I had given her but the man himself who said he was willing to speak to me. We were so pressed for time that we had to say we would do it at the airport. My wife took over and when she spoke to this man he said he couldn't understand why I wanted to contact him. I was not his child. He said my mother was pregnant when they met. I was stunned.'

It turned out that David's problem was partly to do with him using his stepfather's name. His story will be picked up again in chapter five when I discuss the problem of identifying the right name.

It was often the struggle to combat memories of their wives' romantic pasts that led to the stepfathers initiating blazing rows and hostility towards the child, prompting the realisation on the part of the child that they didn't belong. Debra I. of Lancashire was one of them:

'When I was ten years old, my mum and dad (the only one I knew) had another of their giant rows. This time my dad was quite nasty to my mum and he kept saying to her, "Shall I tell her? If you don't then I will." Eventually, after more shouting and lots of crying, my mum told me that my dad wasn't my father. She told me that my father was in the American Air Force and went away after I was born. After finding this out, a lot of memories came back. There was a time when there was only Mum and me. When I had asked about this, my mum had always said that my dad was away in the Air Force, which was true because before my mum married my stepfather, he had been in the RAF, mostly stationed overseas.

'It was strange that when I knew that my stepfather was not my father, it didn't make any difference. He was still my dad; he had been there from almost the beginning of my memory. But from then on, especially when my mum and dad fought – and he was quite a nasty piece of work when roused – I used to dream about going to America to meet my family and that they would welcome me with open arms.

'My stepfather was very strict with me, almost Victorian,

which my mum never agreed with and this caused more rows. At times like this my mind was with my real father who I knew was a caring man. My mother had given me no clues about this, but I'd worried that there was some reason why he had disappeared and had gone to my godmother about it. She said he was a great man; he didn't want to abandon my mum, had begged her to marry him, even went as far as to ask my gran to try to talk her round.

'When he was moved to another base he carried on writing for two years but she never replied. Then he wrote to say he was getting married, but if we ever needed him to let him know.'

Parental disagreement on the raising of children is common when both are natural parents but they have equal rights. The problem is exacerbated and can cause a deterioration of the relationship when there is a stepfather.

'Mum kept taking my side when he shouted at me, which was constantly. He never left me alone for two minutes, always picking on me for this and that. He never actually battered me but he could deal a hefty smack on the legs or behind. The bruises on my arms where he grabbed me were often questioned at school.'

It is not surprising that Debra became what was then called a 'difficult' child:

'I stayed away from school – told lies. By now my stepfather had left and I blamed myself. I thought if I had been his child then he would not have been cross with me all the time, my mum would not have had to stand up for me and there would not have been so many arguments.'

In not wanting to marry the GI this mother had left her daughter with a heavy burden. 'So far I'm no nearer finding him but I feel I must carry on. There must be someone who knows him.' All she has is his rather ordinary name and the fact that he came from Louisiana.

*

63

'Autumn' had suffered from the start:

> 'You cannot believe the cruelty that is stacked on the shoulders
> of a "little bastard". I know I ended up feeling like a dirty, second-
> class citizen and, worse still, was too young to understand why.
> Other mothers didn't want their children playing with "that
> woman's child". Teachers had their own form of cruelty which
> was to give attention and education to the "good and proper
> kids".'

Her situation did not improve when her mother took up with
a married man and produced two more children 'who were little
bastards like me'. Before the third half-sister came along, 'Autumn'
had a stepfather:

> 'Our young lives were sheer hell. This, however, made me
> and my three half-sisters very close. I was told to call the man
> she married "Daddy Len". I suppose I asked too many questions
> like, "Why do I have to say Daddy Len when [my half-sisters] say
> Daddy?" His reply was, "Because, you four-eyed little basket,
> I ain't your dad!" I could never understand why Mum put up
> with the way she was treated.
>
> 'We were always poverty-stricken, never enough food, never
> enough clothes and always cold. We slept three in a bed. Can
> you imagine what it is like to be woken in the middle of the
> night by a huge noise and see a man's fist and arm sticking
> through the door? This was when Len was in one of his terrible
> tempers. We were terrified.
>
> 'There were nights when he would lock himself and my
> mother up and he would beat the hell out of her. What could we
> do? I remember coming downstairs trembling one night to find
> police officers in our back room. My mother had been beaten
> almost senseless, yet she never prosecuted him. I think she put up
> with all of that for a piece of paper that made her a Mrs.
>
> 'I prayed my father would come and get me. In desperation,
> I wrote to the American Embassy and of course got no reply.
> One day, my mum got us all washed and into dresses which were
> clean and tidy. We even had ribbons in our hair and she took
> us to a lovely place. It was full of flowers and shiny, beautiful
> furniture that smelt of polish. To me, as a little kid, it

seemed like a palace. I was so happy until I heard what she was saying. It was a convent and my mum was trying to get the nuns to take us in.

'When I was fifteen, I asked to stay on at school but was told I had to go to work; they needed the money. If only she could have seen that with training I could have brought in far more for her. I proved it when at twenty-eight I went back to college and got my 'O'levels. I was then qualified to train as a nurse and went on to further studies.

'In psychology, I learned to understand what had happened to me and am not bitter about my childhood. Far from it, I think it gave me the guts and determination to live.'

'Autumn' now has a happy home with a very supportive husband and children who are sharing her state of excitement since she has learned that her father has been in touch with an aunt who married his wartime buddy.

Unfortunately, this aunt who lives in the States did not take her father's address when he telephoned, but she knows he has promised to phone again. One can understand the frustration, but at least this call prompted the aunt to send pictures of the father and 'Autumn' can see how much she looks like him.

Stepfathers picking on the child who came into the marriage with their new wife seems common, but a surprising case is one who went to the trouble of falsifying the details of his stepson's birth to make a claim on the child as his natural father. He then would not allow any questions about the real father and made sure that the son did not know that the GI had come looking for him in 1970. With the slimmest of clues, 'a shoulder flash like an ear of wheat which I cannot identify with any unit', this son is now working his way across the United States with a list of people with the same name – as so often happens, quite a common one – trying to find the right man.

Another stepfather has found a different way to be obstructive in order to protect the life he built up with his wife some time after she gave up the child of her wartime romance for adoption:

'My natural mother is not allowed to keep in touch with me by phone – only letter. I have never visited their home. I have a half-brother who is thirty-four. My stepfather does not want him to know about me. He has actually told my mother not to help me find my father.

'I do know that my father was the son of a serviceman and he was in Plymouth in 1944 so must have been part of the forces waiting for the invasion. I have to accept that he may not have survived. It is difficult to find out because I am not sure of the spelling of his last name, only that he was supposed to have come from Texas. I have written an enormous number of letters.'

Someone else held back by the hostility of a stepfather closing off details of his wife's previous life was finally able to obtain her father's name and his home state. She had the advantage of it being the same as a famous General in American history but the delay to her search led only to her father's widow:

'It was clear from my conversation with her that she was totally unaware of my existence. Therefore, I did not want to upset her as he had only died two years ago. Deep down, I would love to know if I have any half-brothers or -sisters, but I do not want to cause pain to the family.'

Many men were full of good intentions towards their stepchild, but often soured the relationship by making the child feel like the odd one out. One man who worked hard to be a good father then spoiled it by dividing that boy from his other children by insisting he not be included in visits to the paternal grandmother. 'My mum would take me somewhere else and that hurt.'

One must bear in mind that stepfatherhood was nowhere near as widespread in the 1940s as it is now. Nor was there the understanding that adjustments had to be made as is recognised today when there is advice and counselling available for men embarking on this role.

The first of the happier notes on stepfathers, more of whom will be found in other chapters of the book, relates to one who married a girl after her mother hid the GI's letters until her daughter was safely engaged to an Englishman. This became an enduring, happy marriage for the couple and from which the child benefited. She now has their full support to try and find her father.

She has discovered that her father married another British girl, but that they are now divorced. However, since her efforts to find him have failed, she is attempting to trace his ex-wife through the GI brides magazine *Together Again* which has a distribution throughout the USA. She hopes this lady will at least have his last address.

Another stepfather willing to help actually took the first step for his 'son' once they had established where his American father lived. He made the initial phone call, established this was the man who had known a certain English girl, and handed the receiver to his son.

Alan H. of Middlesex knew that his grandmother had prevented his seventeen-year-old mother joining her GI after he had sent her the fare. She married an Englishman and Alan became part of the family with two half-brothers. He had not been particularly anxious to find his GI father until his stepfather saw an article in the paper about the organisation TRACE.

By now, he was grown up, married, and himself the father of two sons. His wife took it upon herself to initiate the search and was speedily successful. Alan's father was a childless widower, having married on the rebound when he was turned down by his British sweetheart. Meanwhile, Alan's mother had realised that her marriage was deteriorating and was in the process of a divorce.

Alan's parents have made him 'legal' by finally getting married. However, his mother is finding the adjustment to life in the States no easier than did the original GI brides. Part of this may be due to the fact that life in England has changed dramatically for the better and she finds she has given up more than she expected. 'But, I still love George.'

FIVE

So, Who Is My Real Father?

The pressures of persuasion, the promises of marriage, the pure excitement of the romance – all contributed to the recklessness of the moment! Add to this the deceivers, the outright liars and the unfamiliar accents, and you have some cogent reasons why there were some girls who never really knew the GI's correct name.

However hard it is to accept, Mum's word is not always reliable. She may even have concocted something rather than admit she does not know. This can mean that although the GI's name is on the birth certificate, it does not necessarily confirm he is really Dad. She may have put that name down in good faith, but it may not be his.

The best possible proof was in the 'dog tags', those metal labels they wore round their necks for identification if they fell in battle. But few girls at that time would have been sophisticated enough to demand a look to confirm the name she had been given in fact matched!

The men also wore identification bracelets which were often a gift from the sweetheart they had left in the USA. These could have been passed on as a declaration of undying love to the British girlfriend. They would come in handy when she tried to find him later or passed the bracelet on to their child.

In families, confusion can arise regarding a name, as David C. of Glamorgan discovered. If the child has been adopted either by a couple or the man the mother marries a problem will arise when he first makes contact with the GI.

This turned out to be David's problem. What he did not know

at the airport was that the VA official had already confirmed all the details which identified the man as being the lost father. His confusion was in David's last name. Even when David's wife pinned him down to admit that he had known his mother in England during the war, he still insisted he had not fathered her child, adding the startling accusation that she had been raped by a French Canadian.

David repeated this to his mother who confessed she had made up the story in a quarrel. She then filled him in with details he should have taken to the USA and told him that this GI had been sent pictures of him as a baby.

Left with an unresolved mystery, in March 1988, David felt that for his own peace of mind he had to do something to clarify the situation and returned to Tennessee with his son. They booked into a motel near the American's home, then he telephoned him:

'I chose my words carefully, but it didn't get me anywhere, so in the end, I was blunt and asked if I could come and see him. He agreed and when we arrived we were met by him in the driveway. I was most interested to see what he was like physically and if there was any sort of likeness between us – but there was nothing.

'My main concern was to extract something from the conflicting stories I had been told about this relationship between him and my mother. My grandmother had said he wanted to marry her. He confirmed this but said she rejected him because she didn't want to leave home.'

This is a classic example of how many such marriage plans foundered with no thought to the complications they were to inflict on their child.

The man remembered exactly where the grandmother had lived yet still insisted David's mother was carrying someone else's child. Then, to his utter confusion, David was invited into the house to look at some photographs of the family.

'I didn't see much point, I just wanted to get away from there. I'd been dropped off by taxi so he agreed to take us back to the motel. He began to ask me a lot of searching questions like how did I earn a living, where did I get all my money? Then, he began pointing out local landmarks like the poor

69

farm, explaining that people who didn't have any money used to have to go and live there.'

David was unaware that he was getting a lesson in American social history. During the Depression, those who could not keep up payments on their homes had them repossessed and ended up in the poor farm. Those buildings linger in the mind like a constant threat for those who remember the 'bad times'.

David had not realised that his father was suspicious of his intentions and was testing him to make sure he was not after money. Approaches made by the children of these men are often greeted this way. Many older generation Americans have yet to come to terms with the fact that there are plenty of prosperous individuals outside the USA. All they remember of the UK are the grim war years.

One must also bear in mind that there is a different standard of behaviour. This is not meant to be a criticism but a statement of fact which must be kept uppermost in mind when involved in these searches. It can be the reason why a lot of letters go unanswered. If the recipient has nothing to offer by way of information they may see no point in replying. This does not meant they are being either thoughtless or rude.

British children looking for American fathers or families would do well to remember that it may take time for them to be convinced that the need is purely emotional. Above all, British children wish to identify with their fathers and family. Once this is established, there is a great deal of pleasure in learning about the American half of themselves.

David had not reached that point when this Tennessean dropped him at the motel. Nor did he recognise that the farewell, "If you are ever round this way again, you'll be made very welcome," was a tacit acceptance from this man that he was his son. Instead, he returned to the UK feeling rejected and that his investigation into his background was unresolved.

A few months later, a call came from the lady in Nashville who had remained interested in the case. She had taken it upon herself to make a follow-up call to the GI to see how the meeting had progressed. His comment was that 'they had seemed like a nice sort of family and if she should be in touch to tell them to write'!

Not long recovered from meeting this man and his apparent refusal to make an outright admission that he was the father, David was reluctant to pursue the matter any further. His wife, sensing something more in the words that had been repeated, suggested he at least write a thank you note for the meeting but saying that if they were not related there was no point in continuing any correspondence.

By return post came a letter with an explanation for the odd behaviour. The man admitted the need to make sure David was genuinely his son. Knowing American people better than David, especially from the Midwest, I can understand this man's reaction although I think he was too cautious. Unfortunately, I wasn't there to act as an interpreter.

The conciliatory letter concluded by saying that if David's mother was — then he was definitely his son. David was left feeling that this didn't give him the buzz of satisfaction he had been hoping for, so he made a last trip back to Tennessee to see his father.

He discovered that they were expecting him to stay in the family home, but the drawn out episode of his acceptance had left him preferring to keep his distance so he booked into a hotel. He was greeted with enthusiasm by his father and shown off at 'the store' which is so often a meeting place for locals, almost harking back to Norman Rockwell illustrations. Other people who have visited their fathers in small towns were likewise marched into the favoured place where the locals gather to exchange gossip.

In David's case this 'showing him around' was not extended to the aunts he would have liked to meet; on home ground he only met his father's wife and their children. He was also taken out to view the family burial plots which frequently seem to feature in such visits. At the cemetery he was informed that he could not be buried adjacent to the plot for his father with the stone already in place but that there was one available for him. David declined the offer.

While he will keep up the connection from here on, it is doubtful that David will ever return to Tennessee. This search for his father has ended up costing him £16,000.

*

Glennis S. of Nottinghamshire had a totally different experience of small-town America. When she thought she had found her father in the telephone book of the town which had been his last address, I was asked to act as intermediary.

In case it is mistaken identity or to give the GI a chance to back away, I prefer to start such letters with an apology that I may have the wrong person. However, I then proceed to include enough tantalising details to tempt them to respond. In conclusion a request is made that if this letter has arrived in the home of the wrong person and they happen to know the address of a namesake, we'd like to have it. They are always left the choice of whether they respond to me or the child I have described.

Glennis heard nothing, neither did I. She felt angry and rejected and proposed to go over and confront this man. She also felt it would help her if she at least walked the streets of his home town and knew where he came from.

I urged caution. We already had someone who was not only rejected by his father but threatened with police action if he came near the place. I am also aware that the social scene in small American towns, especially those with little through-traffic, means that a stranger stands out like the proverbial sore thumb. The foreign accent even more so. There would have been no logical excuse for why she was in a town where everyone knows everyone else, including everyone's business.

Fortunately, the silence was broken for Glennis with a letter which explained that the man to whom I had written had done more than pass back the address of a man with the same name: he had actually found her father. What was even more satisfying was that her father had been trying to find her.

They had a wonderful reunion in America during which time she met her half-brother. Both are delighted to no longer be only children. Her father and brother have since visited Glennis in England: 'I do realise how very lucky I am. Someone was certainly looking after me in America.'

Elizabeth C. in Cornwall also thought her search had ended when she found a man whose name and location matched the information she had been given. Her father had been one of the GIs who engulfed the little villages in that area as they trained for the invasion of France. She wrote to the address she found and was unhappy with the reply. The GI was dead and his widow denied that he had ever been to Europe and sent his photograph to confirm this.

Quite forgetting that after forty-five years the locals could hardly be expected to differentiate between one American soldier and another, she accepted that after showing them the photograph they were right in saying she had found her father.

In the meantime, the widow had had the sense to forestall further argument by finding Elizabeth's father. He was delighted enough to come over to claim her. She has since been over to meet the rest of the family and they have begun a transatlantic sharing of each others' lives for special occasions. 'Everyone likes to find their roots and I was determined to find mine for better or worse. It turned out good for me.'

However, this story does prove that whatever confirmation someone may have that the man is their father – he may not be!

Susan C. of Essex had been adopted and therefore needed to find her natural mother before she could begin the more difficult search for her father. Her mother was revealed as a married lady whose husband had been abroad when she met the GI. He had given her the choice of him or the baby when he returned and Susan was sacrificed.

Having rearranged her life, this woman was not particularly pleased to be found and very reluctant to offer much detail of that illicit romance. A name and base was all Susan was given. This appeared to be fine because Susan and her husband belonged to a flying club that took a great interest in the Americans who had flown from their local airfields. This gave her access to the collection of photographs and records of the crews. Examining them, she thought she had come up with a match on the name her mother had given her. At this stage, she panicked over how to make the initial approach and joined TRACE so that I would act as intermediary.

The usual letter starting with an apology for the intrusion was followed with an explanation of why it was hoped we had found Susan's father. I received a letter back saying that he needed to discuss this first with me by telephone. In the call that came from

California, this American sadly explained that much as he would have loved to be the father, he had been shot down over France at the time she would have been conceived.

Susan had to face the fact that either someone had borrowed Bud's name or she had jumped to the wrong conclusion from the coincidence of that same first name in the picture of the crew.

As it was quite a common nickname at time, it doesn't make it any easier for her to follow up. She has now discovered another 'Bud' among the listed air crews but is reluctant to proceed further for fear of another disappointment.

Minor details like missing letters or similarity of first name or last are often the cause of delay or confusion. Mothers who have had a good marriage may by now see their husband as 'Dad' to their child and loyalty to him precludes them from being helpful. Because of this it is sometimes not until that child is adult and usually married that they press harder for the necessary details which will help them find their natural father.

David G. in the Midlands was finally able to put together a flimsy profile of his American father: that he had been a sailor whose ship docked in a northern port; his name which David's mother professed not to be able to spell correctly suggested it was Swedish, and his research showed that the state he had been given was heavily populated by Scandinavian immigrants.

He wrote to the Governor who was willing to be helpful but could find no one listed with that particular spelling. A call to the Swedish Embassy in London produced an alternative. This example of detective work and initiative can be very productive if the ethnic background of the father is established.

A new search of telephone books in the principal towns of Minnesota began. Again, a blank. Finally they had a breakthrough on the home front. A long enough period had elapsed by now to convince the mother that her son and his wife were determined to pursue this search to the end. She 'remembered' the correct name.

There then occurred a series of events for which people searching for their fathers pray. They found David's American uncle. Once they had convinced him they were genuine relatives, he gave them the father's telephone number.

Each time they called they were blocked by an answering machine, hardly suitable for an emotional message. In the end, they left their number with an invitation to call collect.

> 'He finally rang at 3.50 a.m. our time. He said he was half expecting a call sometime and had an idea who we were but not whether he had a son or daughter, or whether the child had survived. He had written to Mum on his return to America but she had never replied.'

They are now in the process of exchanging letters and photographs and adjusting to this extended family scene. For the moment David G. cannot exactly call this GI 'Dad'. Finding him does not change how he feels about the man his mother married: 'He's been the one that always loved me and cared for me.'

The wrong spelling is the premier barrier to a large number of people trying to establish their identity. Helen P. of Cheshire did not realise she had the wrong name when she started out. She even thought she had found instant success with someone, even though he had a different initial. There was at least the hope he was a member of the family. If he was, her search would have been almost at an end. It has been discovered that there are a lot of 'cousinhoods' in the States which have proved helpful.

The person Helen found did not belong to one of these groups nor was he responsive. She realised it would be best to proceed according to her clues and wrote then to the Governor of her father's home state. Again, it was a case where he could not find anyone by that name, but this should not discourage anyone from starting this way because with other families it has proved invaluable.

Helen's almost last resort was to put an ad in the locater column of the *Air Force Times*. While she still did not realise she had the wrong spelling (two letters were missing), her request for information attracted the attention of one of her father's friends. He sent her the correct name and enough details to find him.

He was delighted to hear from her and, just as important, so was his wife. Acceptance by the stepmother is usually more likely if the GI did not marry until his return to America. This lady went even further to prove how pleased she was by inviting Helen over to share the surprise thirtieth wedding anniversary party she was planning for her husband.

The success of her search and entry into her American family was to take Helen into – what has become common with people like her – a whole new phase of life. Settling this last piece of their personal jigsaw into place gives them a supreme sense of confidence. They have proved to themselves that they have overcome what had once seemed impossible. Their whole view of themselves and those around them is now different. There is often the added bonus of going from only child status to becoming enveloped by siblings.

Anticipation of a happy ending can make failure all the harder to bear for those who have every reason to believe that the GI they are seeking is their father. This has been the problem for Andra L. of Worcestershire. The significance of having a GI father did not register until she was adopted by the man her mother married when she was six. Also, like other children in this same situation, she soon sensed it was not a welcome subject for discussion. It was not until she grew older that she felt the need to seek out this unknown figure: 'I wanted to know if I followed him in my ways.' He had written many letters to her mother which had been preserved and she tried the last of them for an address but there was no reply.

Around this time, Andra saw the BBC documentary on GI brides which concluded with a brief mention of the children left behind with unmarried mothers. She wrote to see if the BBC research could be useful to her and that letter was passed to me. She became one of the founder members of TRACE.

She began by combing the Los Angeles directory, listed people with his quite common name, and began a series of letters indicating that she was looking for 'a friend of the family'.

All the replies were negative until 27th October, 1985 when Andra received a letter from a man saying that due to ——'s ill health, the writer would deal with her correspondence. For more than a year Andra exchanged letters but never managed to receive any satisfactory answers or familial claim.

By now, Andra had been put in touch with a 'friend' of TRACE in California who became concerned that she was possibly being conned. 'I wanted to believe her, but there was still a nagging doubt in my mind that perhaps he (the man to whom she had been writing) did know him.'

To make doubly sure, with the help of Shirley McGlade whose group War Babes she had also joined, Andra managed to obtain a copy of the current signature of the man she thought was her father. (This was done by one of Shirley's contacts in the US who sent the man a registered letter, knowing he would have to sign for it.)

When that signature was shown to a graphologist, it was felt that, although there was a span of forty years, there was a satisfactory match to the letters that Andra's mother had received. Since she had still received no confirmation from the intermediary that she was communicating with her real father, Andra decided to go to America and try for a confrontation. 'I took a taxi to the address but lost courage when I reached the house. I was on my own and didn't think I could face rejection. I told the driver to keep going.'

She returned home to write again, explaining that she had had a handwriting comparison made and that it did appear that she had found her father.

A reply came in the form of a solicitor's letter warning her to stop pestering their client.

'I replied that I did not think a handful of letters amounted to harassment and that all I wanted to know was *if* he was my father. I received a letter back stating he was not my father (February 1990). Since then I have left it alone, although I would still like to know.'

I have suggested to Andra that in spite of her 'evidence', she still might have the wrong man since it is such a common last name. However, one can understand that she is too disheartened to make a fresh start on what is just too stressful a subject.

We have encountered such denials before in cases far too obvious to be acceptable. One son has actually been to his father's home area and met the rest of the family. At that time his father refused to see him which was ludicrous because the two of them are so alike that the son has been mistaken for the father in the street.

Someone who was conceived in America when her mother was married to a private in the US Air Force had every reason to assume she was his. Her identity became clouded after she tracked down one of his relatives who told her that her 'father' was sterile. Proof was in the fact that after the divorce from her mother he had adopted children with his new wife. Confronting her mother with this information, she was finally told that the GI's name had only been used for her benefit.

She sadly represents people who have contacted TRACE full of hope but when they have done their sums on the months between their mothers' marriage and separation from the man they thought was their father, they do not provide a logical birth date to be able to make them his child. If the mother then refuses to unlock the door on their identity, they can go no further. As one said: 'I feel more lost than I was when I had his name. Now, I don't know who I am.'

SIX

Just a Photograph Is Better than Nothing

For anyone who has always known both parents, it is not always easy to understand the need to find one who is missing and why it is that people are willing to undergo intense emotional stress in order to do so.

But just to know that 'Dad' was a GI can never be sufficient. A father needs to have a face, an identity to make him real. There are questions which can then be answered: Do I look like him? Is he handsome? Is he tall? What was it about him that attracted my mother?

Even if a child is eventually rejected, however hurtful that may be, they can at least now say something about him, even if it is only, 'He didn't want me.' This is still a better, if more painful, substitute for, 'I don't know who he is.' A photograph can satisfy part of the need; that photograph is 'him'.

But what if there is no photograph? One man travelled all the way to Georgia merely to read and photograph the inscription on a gravestone. It was his only way to establish in his own mind that this man was his father.

However, there is an additional advantage to visiting the cemetery: gravestones can also provide clues. The inscription on one led to a half-sister who has since been traced and is delighted to be found. She will now provide photographs and pass on information about their father.

Several people have chosen to actually have themselves photographed at the gravestone when they are taken there by American relatives. It is a way of establishing themselves as that person's child.

One mother who did manage to hold on to her GI's photograph, saw it destroyed when she was married. Their daughter's only crumb of comfort is the fact that someone in the States may remember her because her American grandmother knew of her birth:

> 'She sent a Christmas card to Mum, but after the first year, that was it. As he was a married man, I doubt I can find out anything more. My main desire though is to see a photograph which would mean everything to me.'

Even if the photographs are not wilfully destroyed, they can disappear over the years. If they are passed on to the child at too young an age, they do not hold enough significance then to be treasured. By the time they are old enough to be concerned – most often as parents themselves – those photographs could have been permanently mislaid.

The tragedy is compounded by then because, besides the emotional value, that photograph may hold important clues in buttons, medals or hats. Also, studying the GI's appearance determines how much his child or grandchildren take after him.

Nicholas Charles who lives in the West Country comments on his heredity:

> 'I've certainly inherited the Italian physique: short and stubby. I have a photograph of my father taken in the war. Now I would love to know him. I do know both he and my mother were nineteen when they met and he was stationed at a camp in Street, Somerset, but so far all I've been able to trace is his military record.'

His mother was one of the women who did not want to go to America. His father sent money to support their child for years after. His mother is now dead, so Nicholas is unable to find out any further details of the romance. Like several other sons of GIs, for the moment he has settled for the next best thing to finding him: compiling a huge dossier of information on his time in England.

Wendy F. of Plymouth did not know much about her father until she found a faded photograph in her late mother's belongings.

Her mother had always refused to talk to Wendy about her father and she was to find out that he did not even know she existed.

The letters gave her a starting point because of the American custom to put the address in the left-hand corner of the envelope. More importantly, in wartime, the men often added their Army service number.

Wendy did not know at that stage that with the number she could have gone straight to the Veterans' Administration headquarters in Washington DC who would have directed her letter to the appropriate area. Instead, she started on the west coast of America, ready to work her way east, from one Veterans' Administration office to another. She was fortunate that, early on in this enterprise, her letter to Colorado touched the heart of the person who read it. His computer pinpointed the state where the GI resided. All she needed to know was the town.

One has to remember that each state is made up of numerous towns, more of them small than large. Each will have its own telephone directory and newspaper. To get through all of them can make for a prodigious feat of endurance which only the very determined will accomplish.

Wendy chose to write her story to the best known city in that state. It had an advice column which was syndicated through several of the area's papers and was spotted by someone who knew her father and who sent her his address: 'He was stunned by my phone call. It was a very long one but neither of us really knew what to say. All I know is I fell in love with his voice as soon as I heard it. I am overjoyed.' She has been able to tell him he has four English grandsons, since when they have come into the many telephone conversations to enchant him with their very English 'Hello Grandad'.

Wendy was afraid of flying and also felt very strongly that she would like her father to meet all of his British family. This was not so simple to organise financially. Then, she was notified he was ill and before she could make up her mind what to do, he died.

'Finding Dad and losing him without actually meeting him has got to be the most poignant event of my life. For a time there, I wished I'd never found him, but now I treasure every memory. I know that he and his wife (who was most welcoming) gave me something so precious. I would not have missed that for anything, no matter what the cost. I was made to feel wanted, not just tolerated. I also discovered why I am the person I am – I am my father's daughter in so many ways, I have such a sense of belonging to them.'

Her father's death was followed by that of his widow, five weeks later. This led to a letter from Wendy's American sister Diane. An excerpt follows:

'I think that the fact that you and he never met is just as painful as losing him . . . You, Bill and the boys held a very special place. We talked about you a lot at the end. I've tried to imagine the pain you must feel, but I do hope and pray that someday the two of us will be able to sit down and talk about it. Now, more than ever I feel a need to see you. It's like I lost a part of myself when Dad died, and now, I finally see that a part of Dad still lives in you. There's a part of me in you as well as a part of you in me!

'I have the consolation of knowing I still have a sister, brother-in-law, four nephews and one great-nephew to get to know someday.'

Some of the people in this book treasure pictures which are often studio posed, showing themselves as a baby, flanked by their mother and GI father. In the case of Gillian B. of Kidderminster, such a photograph is her confirmation of who her father is. Her parents were on the brink of marriage; the reasons why it was cancelled have never been explained to her since any questions to her mother produced instant hostility. Gillian therefore held back from proceeding with the search for which she was armed with the best possible detail – his service number. It was not until her mother died that she sent this to the Veterans' Administration headquarters in Washington DC. They informed her that her father had died in 1980. All she is left with is her birth certificate which shows that before the war he worked as a furniture packer. He has a very unusual first name but for fear of upsetting a widow who may have known nothing about her husband's wartime romance, even though it happened before her time, Gillian feels it would be too unkind to include it here.

Arlene R. of the West Country knew that her mother had changed her mind about joining her father in America. For forty-two years, she treasured her father's photograph, knowing he had pushed her pram down Cornish lanes for the first two years of her life.

When her first attempt to find him failed, Arlene's daughter secretly joined TRACE. Besides giving advice on how to proceed, they have a policy of linking members with a common interest. This can either be that the father was in the same unit, based in the same area, or from the same state or town in the USA.

Arlene was put in touch with one of the successful members and his wife who were going to meet their American family in Maryland. They brought back several addresses of people there with the same name as her father.

One of her letters reached a cousin who responded with news that he was living alone, now in very bad health and confined to a wheelchair. 'The thrill of getting in touch with him was unforgettable.'

It was decided that the most practical way for Dad to meet all the family which by now included his great-grandchildren, was to bring him to England for Christmas which was fast approaching. In spite of the fact that it was a fear of flying that had prevented this man from coming back to England to find out why his old girlfriend had stopped writing, he was now willing to take the chance to meet their child.

That Christmas was to become a poignant memory. Not long after his return to America, her father died. Her only consolation is that the family can now share in the memories.

Starting with a photograph has not proved so simple for Linda G. of Gloucestershire. From it she knows that her first-born son looks like her father. The only other scrap of information she has is that he was stationed at Manston, Kent, in the late 1940s: 'I'm glad I have this memento of him because I shall probably never know him.' This is because she does not have his name; she knows that he was a technical sergeant in the

US Air Force and only knows from the photograph that he is fair-haired. He was sitting with her mother in a deckchair on the sand at a holiday resort. Getting possession of this was not easy. Her maternal grandmother had broken up the relationship between her mother and the GI. 'My mother was put in a special home for my birth. All my father's letters to her were burned by Grandma so that she never received them and thought he had deserted her.'

Her mother's letters to him were also intercepted and therefore never reached America. Human rights was a vision of the future; mothers of that era held full away over their daughters' lives. In this case, it also appears that no one on the staff of this home was inclined to take pity on this poor girl's plight. Perhaps they agreed with her mother that it was best that the lovers were parted and the baby adopted.

Understandably, Linda feels very bitter on her mother's behalf. 'I have to live with this knowledge for the rest of my life.' At least she now knows that her father was a caring man who did try to make contact. Through friends of her mother she has heard that the couple spent various holidays and weekends away over a period of about a year but no one can remember his name. In order to jog some memories, she has attempted to get this photograph published in a US Air Force periodical in the hope that he or someone who was at that base might recognise him, but this has been refused. One cannot understand the editor's reluctance; she is not intent on claiming him as her father until she is sure – therefore it would not be intruding on anyone's past. One has to consider the fact that this man may be desperate for his child to find him. Meanwhile she is at a standstill unless she can find some additional clues.

'Ashley' received the first photograph of her father from her grandmother just before she died. It was very likely that guilt played some part in this because, like so many of the mothers of that time, she had prevented her daughter from marrying the GI. She was willing to take care of the baby so that her daughter could go on with her life unencumbered.

The grandmother also handed over the GI's last address, but a letter there did not find him. However, as in several other such instances, the recipient offered to help. His efforts proved unsuccessful, so 'Ashley' tried an ad in the area paper, carefully worded to avoid offence if her father had a family. She was to discover later there was no need for this discretion because he had told his wife when he married that he had a daughter in England.

The meeting between father and daughter held a touch of fairy story magic: she won a competition – the first prize, a flight to New York. That took the financial burden off the rest of the journey – she was on her way!

When she arrived, her father started with an apology and an explanation that he had really wanted to marry her mother. Several reunions have been prefaced in this way as the fathers want to make it clearly understood what had happened so that they can begin their relationship with their child with no recriminations.

All that was important to her by now was to have found him: 'He did fulfil my image; he's really lovely. I'm so glad.' It has become obvious that, regardless of circumstances, very little can detract from meeting Dad.

Someone who was originally from Stafford and now lives in Australia has been left longing for a photograph of her father because her family in England all insist that her youngest son is his image. She now knows where her father lives, but prefers not to make a direct approach because she is concerned not to disrupt his family life. Some time ago she managed to find her father's address through the Vehicle Licensing Bureau of his home state. At this stage her aunt, who knew him as a friend of the family during the war, offered to take over and act as intermediary. Her pretext for writing was 'for old times' sake', prompted by the fact that the 50th anniversary of the arrival of the GIs in the UK was approaching. There was no mention of the child he had left behind.

There has been no reply. This may be because the man does not wish to pick up on a friendship of his wartime youth – but he might have done had he realised the true reason for this well-meaning letter.

There was a lot of confusion at the start of Elaine H. of Cheshire's life. While her grandmother wanted to keep her in the family, she had a career which meant a lot of travel and the child was fostered out. When she was five, it was decided that she should be adopted:

'Then when I was thirteen, my grandmother appeared at school and told me that my father was a GI and that "Irene", up till then a shadowy figure, was really my mother. She also told me that "Irene" was now married and that apparently her husband did accept me at first but then decided he wanted her but not me.'

In spite of the fact that she was in a happy home, the hurt of being given up festered for years. No one had yet given her any details of her father.

'I was twenty-four when my grandmother and "Irene" came to where I worked but I wouldn't speak to them, I was so bitter. However, as one grows older, one tends to mellow so, eventually, I was willing to forgive and forget but the hurt always remained.'

At that time they were all living in different parts of the country and word came to Elaine that her grandmother had died. It brought home to her that if she wanted to find her GI father, she would first need to locate 'Irene' – which is how she still thought of her mother. 'When I found my mother, she was very relieved. She said she had attempted to find me in 1982.'

Through all of this, Elaine's adoptive parents have been most supportive. Their only concern was that she might get hurt in the search to find her father. All she had to start with was his name and a rough idea of where he might be living. A series of ads were put in the newspapers surrounding the San Antonio area:

'Researcher is looking for a Grady Marshall Riley who came from San Antonio, Texas. He was stationed at Burtonwood Air Base, England, in 1943. Anyone knowing his whereabouts please contact [name and phone number].'

'My phone call from the States came three or four days before Christmas 1987 from Marilyn [one of her sisters]. An aunt had seen the ad in the San Antonio *Evening Express*. It seems they all knew about me but didn't know my name or anything else. One of the first things they asked was what family did I have and what sex were they.'

Elaine was to discover that there was a genetic defect that affected boys in the family; one of her four sisters had already lost a son. They were relieved to learn that Elaine has two daughters.

The American sisters were so keen to meet her that they clubbed together to pay her fare over to them. Before she left she had to arrange for her daughters to undergo tests at a hospital for what was then an almost unknown condition in the UK.

Since then, the Fragile X society has been formed and a little more is known about the condition. The daughters will continue to be tested. They too have met their American aunts, one of whom is now a 'friend' of TRACE.

Most important of all is the fact that Elaine now has pictures of her father, has learned about him from the rest of the family and is delighted at how much she resembles him and her American sisters.

Merilyn K., whose story has been written up in the East Anglia press, started with her father's name and the knowledge that he had been married when he romanced her mother. Because of these circumstances, she also knows that when she was born he was prevented from seeing her and shipped back to the States.

What she did not know was what he looked like nor where he lived. She began her search in 1983 by going through the microfilm record in the American library in Norwich: 'They had five microfiches seething with thousands of names. After six hours, I found him.' Alongside was her father's service number with which she could start to trace where he lived. From that she was notified that he had died some years back and once she knew where, she approached the Salvation Army in one of the Southern states.

In an example of how their response varies from place to place, this particular office went as far as procuring a wartime photograph of her father. With it, Merilyn felt she could approach the widow. 'I wondered whether she would entertain or believe me, but she is really marvellous – a warm, loving woman, who totally accepts my children as her grandchildren.'

Having enjoyed such good fortune with her American family, Merilyn has now set up a support group called The American Connection which operates in her area. They live close enough to each other to participate in what can be very beneficial group therapy.

Hilary F. in Kent knew from her adoptive parents that her father was dead, but nothing else. It was not until she found her natural mother that she learned more:

> 'My mother was a nurse when she fell in love with my father who was a medical officer in the US Army. Their plans for marriage were so complete; she already had her visa to go to America. A fortnight before the wedding, his unit was called to France. Early in 1945, she was notified by the chaplain that he had been wounded in the fighting; his unit had been captured and he died in a prisoner of war camp. He was the youngest doctor to be killed in battle.'

The only way to learn any more about this young man would be through his family. Hilary has few details: 'They were supposed to be something in tobacco.' This does not marry up with the fact that Hilary's mother thought they came from Georgia, primarily a cotton-growing state then. The woman is too frail and ill to be questioned very deeply. It is naturally easier for her to remember the details of their romance and the future they had planned: 'My father was going to specialise in something to do with blood after the war; there was mention of college and Atlanta.'

This may be why her mother believes he came from Georgia. The one other clue which relates to his family is the fact that they suffered a double loss as another son was killed in the Pacific part of the war, the same week as her father.

The story was picked up by the *Atlanta Journal/Constitution* a couple of years ago. The reporter made enquiries at Emory College as well as another medical college in Georgia, but there was no record of Herman Cassey and no response to the story.

Left to right: Christine, who started it all; Norma, still looking for her father; Andrea, looking for her grandfather; Veronica, whose story had a happy ending *(see over).*

ica's father acquires a daughter and two grandchildren all at once.
semary in New England with her husband Doug, her father, and his wife Tess.

Top: David's father then, and now, sitting on the family vault.
Bottom: Phyllis Martin (second from right), friend of TRACE from Corpus Christi, Texas, with Leslie (left), his wife Lesley and daughter Emma, and father Candido.

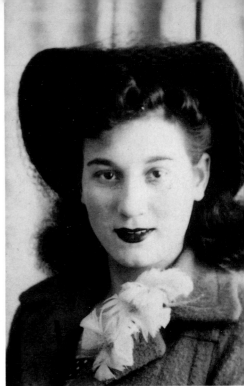

Top: George and Millie then, and *(bottom left)* now.
Bottom right: Linda knows what he looks like, but not his name; her parents met at Butlin's in 1951.

Top left: Michael Roskovitch, killed February 4, 1944, aged 22.
Top right: His grave at Madingley Cemetery, Cambs.
Bottom: Michael's son David, and David's mother Mary.

Top: Justine knows the name of her father (left) but not where he is or why he received this award.

Bottom: Chris on his wedding day, his Cherokee ancestry unmistakable.

Top: James Roscoe Mills at the wedding of his son, also James Roscoe, May 20, 1989.
Bottom left: All Teresa had of her father Henry Obermeyer was this tattered photograph. He is dead, but she will meet his family soon.
Bottom right: Robert Jerome Holbert with his daughter. The son who followed a year later is TRACE member Robert.

Top: Cora meets her father for the first time.
Bottom left: Leone in the US with her father, June 1990.
Bottom right: Anne, who did it all herself, and her husband Terry.

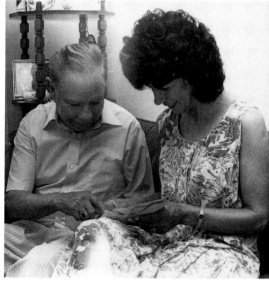

Top: Enrique Cisneros and his daughter Diane in 1944 and 1991.
Bottom: TRACE's indefatigable American 'friend' Harold Ludwig.

Top: Mike (left) with his American brother Dewayne, September 1991.
Bottom: Mike's father, William Ennis Snow, and his grandfather, Daniel Key Snow, Texas, c.1928-9.

Top: Lesley and her son Nicholas at her father's graveside, San Bruno, California, 1990.
Bottom: And just *some* of her new relatives!

This is all Patricia has of her father, Charles Hathaway. He was possibly from Colorado, possibly 1st Company Rangers. She can see the family likeness, and would dearly love to know more about him. Is he dead, as her aunt was told?

If a reader of this book in a tobacco growing state like Kentucky or Virginia recognises the captain's name, or family story, his daughter would be eternally grateful, especially if they could also provide her with his photograph.

Not everyone recognises the value of the information they have on the GI and, as can be seen, they may not have picked up the most important part of it. The name and number are probably the best possible clue to finding him but there are other ways which at first may not seem as obvious but could as easily lead to that photograph which becomes even more precious if they learn that the GI is dead.

After I did a radio programme from Oxford, I was approached by a GI's sweetheart who knew he had been killed in the invasion of France. She and their child have made several pilgrimages to the grave at the American cemetery in Normandy.

What she now desperately wanted was to reach the family he had left behind so they could know about her daughter. In telling me about his youth which included picking fruit in San Jose, California before he enlisted, she omitted to tell me that it was in a totally different area from the address given for his next of kin. Because the years preceding World War II were dominated by the Depression, the shortage of jobs sent some men far afield to find work.

The Mayor of San Jose was extremely helpful but this is now an enormously spread out town, part of what is known as Silicon Valley. He checked with the oldest school because American high schools have a year-book in which there are pictures of the graduating class. Had this GI been listed, there would have been the precious photograph they wanted in England. Unfortunately, he was not there.

A private investigator was employed by this lady. He found a sister, now a widow, living in a small town in Arkansas which was the address given when she had been listed on his Army papers as 'next of kin'. This sister was overjoyed to discover she had family in England and immediately planned to visit the daughter and grandchildren her brother never lived to see.

David E. in Sussex always wondered as a child why his mother carted him off annually to the American cemetery in Madingley. The stone where she left flowers had a 'foreign' name which assumed no significance for him.

It was not until he was forty-one that she blurted out at a dinner party that she had been taking him to visit his father. Up till then, the only 'father' he had known was his mother's second husband who had made him suffer a traumatic childhood to such an extent that he had developed a stutter.

It was therefore with some interest that he now discovered that his father had been Mike Roskovich, a legend in the 306th Squadron of the USAF, who was the first man to complete twenty-five missions in a Flying Fortress.

His mother was only sixteen when she met her hero. After she discovered she was pregnant, her parents persuaded her not to tell him. Instead, they encouraged her to hastily marry the English boyfriend who had been a persistent suitor. While she agreed (as has been seen, girls rarely argued with their parents then), this marriage had little chance to succeed when there was a suspect, 'premature' baby.

After her divorce, David's mother felt she was now free to find her first love and tell him about their child. Her investigations into his whereabouts (he had been sent back to the States for officer training then returned to the UK) led to the tragic discovery that he had been killed in an off-duty plane crash.

When she finally decided to tell her son the truth about his parentage, she felt it would be better to present him with a photograph of his father. Most logically, the best place to obtain one was from the organisation Friends of the 8th. In approaching them she solved the mystery of who had been leaving flowers on the hero's grave.

From their collection of photographs of the historical exploits of the 8th Air Force, they were astonished at the resemblance between Mike and his son. Therefore, in May 1987, David was invited to lay a wreath at the annual Memorial Day ceremonies at the American cemetery in East Anglia. There he was presented with several photographs of his father:

'It was wonderful to learn that he seemed to have an abundance of guts, plus a sense of humour. Additionally, my previously

supposed father was five foot six and both my sons and I are
six foot three which had always puzzled me a bit.'

Sue F. of Avon has not yet been as fortunate as David. She
desperately would like that similar link with a dead father. 'He
was killed in action in Belgium in 1944. My mother failed to
follow up on the opportunity she had at that time to contact
his family.'
One has to have some understanding for a young woman of
that era. It would not have been an easy task to write to tell a
young man's family she was unmarried but pregnant. In her case,
he had been called away to battle too fast to implement the plans
they had made, but he made sure the expected child would be
supported with a government allowance.
There were pictures and letters but they were destroyed by
the jealous man who became Sue's stepfather. This leaves her
with very little but a fragment of his service number which has
not proved enough to track down his family. 'I know he had a
sister. If I could make contact with the surviving family it would
be wonderful.'
Several friends of TRACE have searched telephone directories
at random, but no one has yet found a listing with the last name,
Chamless. This is frustrating because usually an uncommon name
proves a great advantage.

One who knew her father's home town, took a chance on a name
that looked similar but was spelled differently. She had found her
half-brother who informed her that their father had died some
years eariler. He was willing to build a relationship with her:
'Since then, we have exchanged photographs. I now have pictures
of my dad as well as of my brother and his family.'
This is a secret that has to be kept from the widow who did
not know that her husband romanced Lily's mother. This is
no isolated incident. There have also been many cases where
the British sibling has been made welcome even if the father
is dead. Uncles in particular seem the most relieved. This is
possibly because their brothers had confessed to them about the
child left behind.
The majority of GI children conducting this search, work hard

to be as discreet as possible and thus avoid causing any domestic chaos in America. Sometimes they are forced to take chances owing to the lack of co-operation from their mothers in the UK.

One woman who had been promised her photograph when she was twenty-one found that when that time came her mother put her off:

> 'She has since refused to tell me anything more. All I have is my father's name. The first is unusual, the last too common to find except for the fact he was supposed to have been a professional footballer before he went into the services. He is the only black man my mother went out with.'

This has left her with an extra burden which was recognised in a school playground in an area where there had once been a large number of GIs of all races: 'I can still remember playing with this little dark girl. She said to me one day, "You are the same as I am, but you are white." '

This child had already realised that this was going to make a difference to her life.

SEVEN

Something You Can't Hide

Regardless of whether they were raised in the family or adopted, the children of white GIs could grow up with no more than the slur of their illegitimacy. And although they might cruelly be labelled 'Yankee Bastard', they could outgrow this, especially if they moved away from their home area.

The problem for the dark-skinned children was that even if they were adopted, they did not blend with the Anglo Saxon natives. Up until 1958 in Britain, to be anything but pink-skinned was unusual.

There were some black people around the ports; Liverpool, for instance, has had a black community going back further than both world wars. London too, with its more cosmopolitan mix, showed the occasional dark face, but it was rare enough to be commented upon. Such people would have been assumed to be of Indian, rather than African descent, in fact the term then used for a person of mixed race was 'half-caste', a phrase which originated on the Indian subcontinent.

Perhaps because of the absence of blacks, Britain was not a colour-conscious nation in the 1940s. This is not to suggest that it was all sweetness and light. There were cases of controversy, but incidents like the one which involved the famous West Indian cricketer, Constantine, being refused a room in a smart London hotel were rare. There was still a vast hinterland in the UK through which a black person had yet to pass. They were as unknown as Americans which meant that when the troops who were Negro, Mexican or Red Indian arrived, they received the same classification from the British as the whites. They were all GIs.

The locals did not realise how very unexpected this was to the black Americans, especially those from the segregated southern states. There, they had grown up with such a strict division between black and white, it covered every aspect of their lives from birth onwards. Places were labelled. I remember my own personal horror in the late Forties when I first arrived in the south and saw 'black' and 'white' signs on toilets, water fountains and libraries. I also learned first hand what it was like to suffer racial prejudice when I was shopping in Illinois with a deep Florida suntan.

The black GI found no such restrictions in the UK. However, the welcome they received from the locals, especially the girls, did not go down well with the white Americans. Their abhorrence of this is dramatically illustrated in a dance hall scene in the film *Yanks* when violence erupts.

For some reason the white GIs were not quite as bothered by the girls going out with the dark-skinned American Indians or Mexicans, but, in any case, they were fewer in number.

The babies of these associations were not so easily explained away by the excuses which covered other illegitimate births. Consequently, especially where there was a concentration of black troops, many of these dark-skinned babies were quickly relegated to local authority homes from which they were not as readily rescued by adoption.

Both Richard N. and Leon Y. were raised in baby homes in the Somerset area and were featured in the Harlech TV documentary, *Brown Babies*. Richard had the disadvantage of knowing that his father's name is one of the most common for black people in the United States. This particular GI was stationed at Martock and met his English girlfriend at a local dance. It was the GI's involvement in a motor cycle accident which was the cause of him being sent back to the States prematurely.

Leon's story was in the book *When Jim Crow Met John Bull* by Graham Smith. His first step was 'Honicote', a home commandeered by Somerset County Council for the overflow of dark babies.

When he was five, he went to Wellington Home. When he

grew older, he was moved yet again to another boys' home. This stands out in his mind because: 'I can remember that my mother came to visit me when I was about thirteen but never again [in his childhood].'

It may well have been that because he saw his mother's desertion of him as relating to his colour, his illegitimacy did not dawn on him until he was visiting a friend in his teens: 'His mother remarked, "Pity about you lot in the war." It was at this point I realised that I was born out of wedlock.'

An article in the *Guardian* in 1984, referring to Graham Smith's research into black GIs in the UK, made Leon want to know more about himself. He contacted Social Services to see if he could find his mother.

> 'We were reunited within two months and I learned a few details about my father. He was based at Wells, Somerset, before D-Day and knows I was named for him. He was a corporal. I don't necessarily have to meet him but I would like to know the family history.'

While the reasons are slightly different, the singer Iris Williams was also put in a home because of her colour. Her mother, a married lady with a husband away at war, found that her husband was prepared to accept the child until he saw her dark skin.

Not surprisingly, when she was small, Iris felt unwanted: 'I was sad and angry. I couldn't understand it. You feel unloved – why did your mother give you away; that there is something wrong with you – and all that nonsense!' She was fostered at the age of five: 'I remember being very excited at the prospect of this new mummy and daddy coming to take me to their home.'

It was through her foster mother's love of music that Iris began to sing: 'At school, I had music lessons but I had to leave when I was fifteen. I went to work in a glove factory.' An understanding boss who had obviously learned of her magnificent voice agreed to let her take time off for those lessons. This led to a scholarship at Cardiff College and the rest, as they say, is showbiz history. 'What I did not appreciate then, but I do now, was that Bronwyn [her foster mother] could well have done with me working and bringing in some wages, but she didn't stop me studying music; she encouraged me.'

Iris had a very happy childhood in her foster home but at eighteen wanted to establish her full identity. To do this, she had to find her natural mother who she hoped would be able to tell her about the American father she knew she had.

A discreetly worded ad in the local paper was recognised by the one brother in whom their mother had confided details of her wartime romance. Through this, Iris met the English side of her family. What was fascinating was the fact that although she undoubtedly inherits her dark skin from her GI father, she, her mother and the other siblings all match facially.

So far, Iris has not been able to find her father. She has very few details to work on but, as this book goes to press, may have found his brother in Cincinnati. If this leads to him, he is going to have a surprise when he discovers what has happened to his British daughter and that she sings for American presidents. Iris is constantly invited across the Atlantic to give concerts for the President Ford Foundation. She keeps hoping that one of these days she will be going over there to meet her father.

In dramatic contrast, 'Beatrice' was not so lucky when she was fostered. It appears that no one was advised that her bad behaviour which antagonised so many people very possibly arose from an understandable sense of insecurity.

She had begun by being privately fostered on week days while her mother worked to support her. Then the woman gave up, abandoned her child and emigrated, address unknown.

One must have some compassion for this woman given her situation. She had been taken out to dinner by a friend of a friend; at the end of the meal, he drugged her coffee. The apology for the rape that she was not aware had taken place was stuck in her handbag which she found when she came to in a taxi. 'Beatrice' was the result of this humiliating experience and one can see that this would have been very difficult to deal with.

The authorities put 'Beatrice' in a Dr Barnardo's home where she found she was shunned by the other children for being neither black nor white. At first, she knew nothing of her personal history other than her father's name and assumed he had deserted her mother: 'I was thirty-four before I was told about the rape.'

Since then, she has thought it through to the extent that she feels that her father – Roscoe – showed a sense of conscience in leaving her mother the note of apology. This was followed up by a visit to her when she was in the hostel having the baby. He left her £25 (quite a considerable sum in those days). One assumes it was towards the expenses.

'Beatrice' would like to know what else she inherits from him besides her dark skin; perhaps the iron determination which has enabled her to survive the unhappy childhood in which she was passed through a succession of foster parents alternated with homes until she felt like an unwanted parcel.

'Beatrice' is now a trained nurse, and has the compensation of a good marriage and satisfying motherhood. She wishes her children had grandparents to enjoy them. She has managed to find her mother's sisters who are unwilling to discuss this family scandal, so she is no nearer learning anything else which might help.

A proportion of fathers who knew about their child, kept in touch with the mother for some time after their return home. This could have been founded on a mixture of guilt or pride in consorting with a white girl, as much as parental concern. The majority, however, would have realised that at that time a black/white marriage would not have worked. One of the mothers commented that her GI had said he did not think she would be happy in America. This was an understatement, especially if they were going to a southern state. They would never have been able to sit down in a restaurant together, let alone find an acceptable place to live. Like 'Beatrice' in the home, they would have been deemed undesirable by both races.

There were some marriages, but most of these brides did not fare well. In fact when I was researching for *Sentimental Journey* there seemed to be no such bride at all. I had to assume few of those marriages had lasted. Then, much too late for inclusion in that book, I did learn of one, still going strong in Texas, so it follows that there must have been more. Nevertheless, one must assume that in the majority of cases, even after marriage, there were second thoughts.

*

Jill S. of Hampshire has her father's colouring. She was left to be raised by her grandmother after she advised her daughter not to follow her black GI to the States.

> 'My father kept in touch with me for years, but it was intermittent. He sent birthday cards and gifts, then there would be a lapse. He used to write and say he wanted me to visit him in America, but when I wrote back to say I'd come, I didn't hear from him again for some time.'

It was not until she went to America with her English husband on a business trip that Jill realised she had probably done better by being raised in England. They flew in to the south which, twelve years before, was officially integrated but still not used to too much of such a social mix. Jill's husband is white and their children vary in skin shade. Their arrival at the airport caused a commotion: 'They stared at my husband and me and our children all the way through Atlanta airport.'

Some fathers who had not married the mothers, made strenuous efforts to have their children sent to them: 'He didn't want me; he was more interested in the baby and wrote to say he had arranged for a stewardess to accompany him back, but I wouldn't let my son go.' She did send pictures of the child over the years but there came a time when they were returned, 'address unknown'. It is now proving impossible to find the man and let him know how well their son has turned out.

What is something of a surprise to these fathers who were raised in a segregated world, except for their adventure in the UK, is how well their children have done here. This does not mean that these children have been without problems along the way. They have often fought through setbacks to reach that success.

Robbie W. from East Anglia had a mother who made him feel proud of his colour, insisting that:

> 'We [he had a sister from the same father] would always have to be better than the next person to even be accepted as being equal. It wasn't always that easy. I did not only feel different but was obviously made to feel different by the normal evil of children. I certainly suffered a lot of torment as a child.'

As these children grew up, the social attitude was changing in the UK – not always for the better!

Robbie's father was a career serviceman who came to the UK in the early Fifties and was with his mother for some time. He was then posted to Florida which was a sharply segregated state. He realised that there was no way that he could have a domestic life with a white woman and their children and asked his base chaplain to write and explain the situation. Robbie's mother had no way of understanding this and saw the letter as an excuse for the GI's desertion. It became a closed subject of conversation.

'Until the age of nine or ten, although never told it, I thought my father was dead. I first started looking for him when I was sixteen, unfortunately for the wrong reasons – mostly anger at the shameful treatment I felt my mother had received. I think I wanted to punish him, and in my immature way, I made some half-hearted effort to find him.'

He approached the search in earnest when he was twenty-six, trying about twenty different associations such as the US Army enlisted records and the Chamber of Commerce near his father's base in Florida. All of this was unsuccessful. Then his secretary heard something about TRACE on the radio and gave him the address: 'I was often tempted to give up – especially as my family [mother and sister] seemed against my search. I must say, TRACE always prompted me to continue.'

Eventually, at their suggestion, he tried a research consultant who sent him the description of someone whose details and name matched his father's. Robbie panicked, not sure how best to approach this person and fearful that if he did it wrong it would ruin any chance of a proper reunion.

The son of a 'friend' of TRACE, who was Robbie's age, volunteered to make the intermediary telephone call. There followed several stressful weeks in which only the telephone answering machine responded. Finally the father was reached. He is delighted to be found and they are in the process of catching up on the lost years by letter, before they actually meet.

*

Jim K. of Norfolk had known absolutely nothing about his natural father. His mother was already married when he was born and he was successfully absorbed into the family:

> 'I had one elder sister and brother and there was a large gap between our ages. I don't remember being treated any differently. It was when I was eleven and asked why I had black, curly hair, but never got an answer, that stands out. To this day, my mother has never told me anything about my father. I can remember only one incident at school when a girl called me a black B, so I hit her with a ruler; that's the first and last time I ever hit a girl. I was lucky at our school, there was no racial prejudice.'

It was not until Jim applied to join the Army when he was eighteen that there was the question of who was his father:

> 'I needed a passport for overseas duty. I had to produce a birth certificate and I hadn't got one. They sent me home on weekend leave to find out if my name was really the one I'd given and if the details my mother had filled in on the forms were correct. My mother assured me they were and I was eventually given a passport on my mother's first husband's marriage certificate.'

No further query into his background came up until Jim met the girl he was to marry. She asked questions about his past and family and he had to tell her that he didn't know anything about this. It did not prevent the marriage and it was when Jim was moving some personal papers into their new home that he came across a small birth certificate. This showed a different name for his father. 'We talked about it, rejected the idea of finding this man and got on with having a family.' It was not until 1987, at the age of forty-two, that Jim found out where he came from:

> 'My father had registered me himself. Therefore, we thought he must have wanted me. We had his Army number and set about trying to get in touch with Transatlantic Children's Enterprise [TRACE] and we made contact with a lovely lady in Wales called Sophia Byrne. She really got the ball rolling. [She wrote

a letter to the father in Jim's name.] We must have been one of the lucky ones; it only took a few months.

Sophia was as overjoyed as Jim was when on 8th August, 1987 he received a letter:

'I can't describe how I felt to receive a letter starting with "Dear Son" and ending with "Your loving father". I sent photographs of my family and he was thrilled to know he had got a grandson and told me I have a half-sister who knew about me and always hoped that one day I would contact him. He told me he would have liked to have taken me with him but regulations stopped it. He sent photographs of himself and it's like looking in a mirror. I would dearly love to see him, to be able to talk to him, to ask questions, just to hug him.'

Jim was to discover that his father had carried a picture of his British baby for all those years. It must have been like a confirmation of a totally unreal experience once he had returned to Alabama. Had he brought Jim's mother and her two white children and their baby to live there they would have had a very difficult life.

With a first name of Lavern, a man in Northamptonshire knows it has to have come from the American half of his family. He started off full of hope with information on them that stretched back to grandparents. With this, a 'friend' of TRACE in Texas followed up every source of the details he sent her which included the fact that his grandfather was supposed to have been a dentist. She contacted the Alumni Association of those few colleges there that would have admitted blacks at that time but no one by that last name has been found. Lavern has to assume that the original details were incorrect or possibly embroidered upon.

Leo M. in Lancashire thought the fact that he carried his father's middle name of Junius gave him a good start. Although he was legally adopted by his mother's husband when she married, his natural father sent him birthday cards and photographs for eight years. It was not until he finally began the search for him as an adult that Leo discovered that his father had died in 1986. He would like to learn if there is any family and also where the GI is buried so that he could at least go to the cemetery and pay his respects.

His father's last name was hyphenated, which makes it more unusual in the USA, and he knows that he came from either North or South Carolina but, short of searching every telephone book in that area, he has no other clues as to where his father lived.

'I was going to be put up for adoption because my mother was only seventeen,' says Dennis B. of Oxfordshire, 'but my grandfather made the decisioin that my mother could keep me and bring me home.' Until he joined TRACE, Dennis had always assumed that his 'foreign' looks were because his father was Spanish/Italian. This is only part of the early confusion, not helped by being raised in a house with grandparents as well as a mother. His mother had told him that his father 'went away' to Dunkirk. This military event was a retreat and took place before the United States came into the war. Since the American was attached to one of the medical units in the Oxfordshire area, it is probable that he followed the invasion forces into France. Dennis has checked the military cemeteries to make sure his father was not a casualty. He cannot be certain, however, that he has the correct spelling of what looks likely to be a Mexican name. The fact that he comes from Kansas makes this a possibility because a colony of Mexicans settled in that state more than 150 years ago.

Using the name he has been given has not led Dennis to find the man through the usual sources like the Vehicle Licensing Bureau. It is still likely, therefore, that with a variant spelling he might still find his father somewhere in Kansas who could be so proud of three English grandchildren who have done very well academically.

As so many of these people were given Anglo Saxon first and last names, their olive skins and liquid brown eyes made them seem even more misplaced.

Pauline Natividad of Southampton was named after her GI

father at his request and thus had the advantage of a foreign last name to go with her dark looks. Her only problem, when she started to look for her father, was that she had been told that she had also been given her first name to match his.

After the war, her mother married an Englishman and had more children which must have made Pauline feel very much like the odd one out. 'These sisters had a mum and dad, but I only had a mum. I called my stepfather "Uncle" and hung on to the fact I had my own "Daddy Paul", which my mother and grandmother had always called him. Then when Pauline was eight, her mother died: 'I was taken back to live with my grandparents and when I was about ten, my granny gave me three photographs of my father and showed me that his name was on my birth certificate.

'During the years I lived with my grandparents, they and my aunts all said that Paul had been killed at the end of the war.' This was the usual justification for the GI who did not come back to claim mother and child.

When both grandparents were dead, the urge to find someone in her American family was very strong. Pauline felt that: 'Even if my father had died, there must be someone somewhere in the United States.' She began her search by going to Southampton library, which has a very good selection of US phone books, and looking for anyone with the same last name.

'I copied about 150 "Natividads" in several states. After unsuccessfully contacting two "Natividad" families I then discovered my father's name was Pilar, not Paul. On Thanksgiving Day, 1988, I called a Victor Natividad in El Paso. I had a strong feeling about this one and asked if he knew a Pilar V. Natividad. Victor told me that Pilar was his father. How did I react to the news? It's almost indescribable. At first, I felt absolutely stunned, then sheer elation and joy. He had been alive all the time. I was on cloud nine and still am. I'm so very glad I've found my dad. Finding him and my new brother and sister and their families in El Paso has filled a void in my life. Certainly I was born here in England and am British, but I am also half Mexican. After forty-four years, that dark-haired, olive-skinned little girl knows who she is and it's wonderful. In his first letter, my dad said, "From the bottom of my heart, I thank you for your continuous effort in locating me." '

Pauline was to discover that her father had been wounded in the fighting and sent back to a rehabilitation centre in England to recover. (There were several military hospitals set up in the UK to deal with the casualties of the fighting in France.) While at one of these rehabilitation centres, he saw her at the age of three months. So she had been deliberately misled by being told he had died in the war. She also found out that her father had promised to marry her mother although this would have been difficult because he already had a wife and child in El Paso.

Whatever her father's plans might have been, when the war in Europe ended he, like many GIs, may have expected to return to the States via the UK to implement them. This was not to be; in the main they were shipped directly home from France. Pauline's father wrote to her mother for a year but never returned to Britain.

Pauline had two friends at the City Bus Company where she worked who had encouraged her through this search. When they spread the news of her success, the staff took up a collection so that she could spend Christmas with her father. As there was a family wedding planned for that time, he came up to El Paso from his home in Benson, Arizona: 'I will always remember him standing there to greet me.' Immediately she was engulfed in a totally new experience of Mexican living which included their Catholic faith.

'This is very important in their lives. We went to church and I sat there with people who all looked like me. I no longer stood out with my dark skin. It was a wonderful feeling. It's fascinating that they all speak Spanish then switch to perfect English.

'The wedding was that of my niece Zulema to Armando. They played Mexican music at the reception and pinned money on the bride's dress.'

Since then she has been back for a second wedding and to meet even more of the family. 'One of my uncles has built a hacienda in Arizona.' It was a far cry from the suburbs of Southampton. Also on this visit Pauline went to her father's home in Benson, Arizona, where he had received his phone call from her. There she met his second wife to whom she had been a complete but, fortunately, pleasant surprise. Then they all went on to visit an aunt and uncle in California who are the pride of the family. She now shares the pleasure of his accomplishment: 'This was an underprivileged family of sixteen children. Now, my uncle is the Mayor of Pico Rivera.' Equally important was the fact that her uncle was able to supply her with details of the family which go back two generations. She is now totally absorbed by her Mexican heritage.

Chris S. in the Midlands would love to share such a cultural experience. It would not be difficult since he so unmistakably descends fròm American Indians with his Cherokee father's dark looks which have been passed on to his daughter. This has caused her to have problems at school; today's society is not as tolerant of colour as it was when her GI grandfather came over in the early 1940s.

Chris too admits to having suffered some harassment in his childhood which he feels toughened him up. Given his bulky size, it is a wonder anyone dared to fight with him. His search for his father has been motivated by his daughter's problems and her wanting to know why she is different from her peers. When he collected her from school some months ago, he inadvertently added to her woes when they saw his dark skin. She began to be taunted about the fact that her father was 'black'.

It was not until her mother protested to the teacher that she discovered that he too had assumed this. To his credit, he then gave the class a lesson about Red Indians which helped the situation.

Nevertheless, this playground strife propelled Chris's wife into taking over the search for his father: 'We have an affidavit from him admitting paternity just before Chris was born in 1944. On it, he also agreed to make an allowance for the baby and pay all expenses, but there was no contact after that.' What makes this wife angry is that she feels the GI started something that he doesn't want to finish. They are sure they have found his address, but their letters have not received replies. He has even ignored the one from the child begging to know if he would acknowledge or deny he is her grandfather.

This is all very distressing for this little dark-skinned girl who could be said to be suffering for the sins of her grandfather.

Confirmation that this man is Chris's father has in fact been made with the help of Shirley McGlade's War Babes group. She arranged to get a signature for a recorded delivery letter. As Chris is a policeman, he has the facilities for a professional comparison with the one on that affidavit. It came up positive.

What makes the situation even more distressing is that his child is suffering a depleting illness. She was dangerously underweight until homeopathic medicine restored her. Chris and his wife refuse to give up and letters continue to go out from Dudley, Worcestershire, to Oklahoma on a regular basis.

Children looking for dark-skinned fathers find it difficult to make contact in many cases because it seems that these men do not keep in touch with their old units in the same way as many of the other GIs.

There is, however, a National Association for Black Veterans and one for Indian Affairs. Neither seems to have the facilities to help nor the ability to understand my involvement in tracing these families.

When I visited Washington DC in November 1989 to try to get some on-the-spot information, I was met with surprise that, as a white person, I was so active in these searches. The attitude to colour does seem to be different in America. Ethnic groups seem to keep much more to themselves. This is illustrated in a letter from a member of TRACE born of a British mother and black GI in the States and then abandoned: 'I find myself dwelling on the circumstances of my life and how it has affected my ability to form relationships with people. Finding my father would be the last piece of the puzzle.' 'Bonnie' was put up for adoption:

'I was very fair with straight hair as a baby, but obviously not white which is why the first family I was placed with gave me back. In 1954, there was no interracial adoption and segregation and discrimination were very much alive.' (I might add that this was in a Northern state.)

'Bonnie' went back into foster care until she was adopted by a black family. When she grew up, contrary to what has happened to the majority of children of black GIs in the UK, she has a black husband and her social life seems limited to people of her own colour.

To protect her adoptive mother who wants to pretend that she is her natural mother, 'Bonnie' has blurred the circumstances of her birth and background to her friends there.

Even though the facilities for a search for a father ought to be more accessible as she lives in the USA, so far she has had no luck. It has made her very despondent. Because of this and the fact that, where possible, TRACE likes to link people with some similarity of situation, she has now been put in contact with 'Beatrice' and they have begun a special friendship.

'Bonnie' would also possibly benefit from meeting a more recent member who is a psychotherapist and admits that this struggle with her true identity is difficult to work through. She is the result of a black/white romance of the early Fifties. Once her mother learned that the GI was married, she legally adopted her child to prevent him making good his intention to take the baby back to America.

Now she has her own home and a successful career, she says:

'I want nothing more from him other than to meet him; it will be like discovering another part of me. I have respect for his family and the life he has created for himself and wish that any contact we may have does not cause anyone distress.'

The majority feel this way and only wish that their fathers would understand and try to find them.

EIGHT

Daddy Doesn't Live
Here Any More

Maybe not – but he did marry Mummy, which means these children have a different status from the others in this book. They can, in certain cases, claim to be American and if they are natural-born citizens they will of course have become one in their own right. One might think that this would give them a better opportunity to locate their fathers, but it has often not been so.

For example, there is the question of the legitimacy of the marriage. A GI may have married without the permission of his commanding officer. Such ceremonies were often a hurried registry office affair with starry-eyed-in-love (and possibly pregnant) girls who may have given in to the persuasion that there was no need to have 'official' approval or wait for 'all that paperwork'. How could she have known that this was a clear signal that the GI had something to hide? That official approval was not handed out until his records had been checked? Naturally, if those records showed that there was already a wife that he had conveniently forgotten, his request for this marriage would be vetoed.

The dependence of his parents on his financial support would also show up in the shape of regular deductions from his pay. This was common at the time if the GI came from a poverty-stricken area yet to recover from the Depression. Their Army pay could represent the first regular and reliable wages they had ever earned. Many willingly made sure it helped their families. Under such circumstances, the CO or chaplain would rightly voice doubts and discourage them from also supporting a wife.

This may have accounted for the more responsible of these men preferring to promise to send for the girl later. If he did not, she can now count herself lucky she was not pitched into the deprivation that some of the GI brides met.

Another reason for officers to discourage marriages was because they knew that at that time the quota which allowed British immigrants into the USA was minimal. This situation was not changed until an Act of Congress in December 1945 allowed the brides mass entry if they were officially recognised. Even after this there were still medical restrictions against certain ailments more common at that time. This could well have been what 'Penny's' father discovered:

'When he left me and my mum in England, he was a happily married man determined to sign on in the Army for another year. Then why did it all go wrong when he returned to the USA? I know my mother was very ill at the time and unable to travel. [She was recovering from TB which was very prevalent in the 1940s.] Instead of understanding the situation, he divorced her.'

Last-minute panic was another reason for the deterioration of a marriage. Some of the people in this chapter arrived at the GI bride disbursing centres as babes in arms. Disbursing centres were either the barracks at Tidworth on Salisbury Plain which had housed the invasion forces or the Carlton Hotel which had been a rest and recreation centre for American servicemen on leave. Here the women were checked for vaccinations, asked to hand in their ration books and allocated a ship. All very frightening for these young women, many of whom had never really taken charge of their children. If they now found the task too enormous without their mum, they decided to go home again. Such teenage fears are not so easily admitted to their now grown-up children asking awkward questions.

The men also had time for second thoughts before the women were shipped out which would have related to regret or the circumstances of their arrival back home. Therefore, boarding a GI bride ship did not guarantee the British girl a welcome on the other side. The accumulated embarrassment, bitterness

and fury of an experience like this make it hard for these GI
wives to discuss the failure of the romance that turned into a
sour and often brief marriage.

'Rene's' mother received a telegram from her husband *en route* to
tell her he had found someone else. This traumatic shock came in
spite of the fact that she had had a hearts and flowers wedding with
dress, ring, and blessings from his family. 'Rene' knows that she
will only get the answers to what went wrong from her father.

The first contact she made was unsatisfactory. He saw no
sense in picking up on their relationship. She was devastated
but determined not to allow this to happen and began a series
of telephone calls, redialling every time he hung up. 'I shall keep
on writing to him. I'm sending him a birthday card. It's something
I've waited all my life to do; he's not going to stop me from doing
that now.'

'Jenny's' mother married in hope with the classic one page,
one bridesmaid and rose bouquet wedding. She represents the
contingent of GI brides who arrived in the States with a child
in arms, only to be horrified by what they found. While some
had more sense than to expect to be swept into the luxury of
Hollywood, they had every right to assume that such a seemingly
rich country would have basic amenities for everyone: 'They didn't
have proper furniture; the bed came down from the wall.' She had
arrived in a family so poor that when her second child was born
she had to go to a charity hospital. It seems that soon after that,
she managed to get herself and the children back to England.

'Jenny' is finding that her mother does not wish to discuss
this traumatic period of her life and she left all the pertinent
documents relating to it there. This is causing her daughter
problems; all she has is her father's name, and he is not
responding from his last address. Bearing in mind the change
for the worse in certain sections of New York City, this is hardly
surprising.

'Jenny' cannot even take the usual route to finding him via
the Driving Licence Bureau which can often provide the current
address. New York is one of the few 'closed' states and requires
documents to prove that such enquiries are genuine. Hers

are somewhere in America; if she found them, she'd probably find her father.

Her only compensation at the moment comes from the Salvation Army who will help her because she is the legal issue of this man – apparently they are willing to take her word for it.

The Salvation Army were equally kind to Cora M. of Surrey. She too had sailed with her mother on a GI bride ship. They had gone to live in upstate New York with her father's large, voluble, Italian-speaking family.

Assimilation into such a different culture proved hard for many of the British girls. Pregnancy was to provide one of the escapes. Husbands often generously gave in to their request to 'go home' to have the baby in the hope that this one visit back would convince them of the advantages of American life.

Cora's mother never returned. The children grew up in England carrying their very unusual foreign name and their mother built a new life.

'Turchetti was not that easy to pronounce! I kept the name but because of a stepfather I adored and the fact that I felt he would be hurt if I wanted to find my natural father, I did not do anything about searching for a long time. I always thought there would come a time in my life when I would.

'What I didn't realise was that the very sudden death of my stepfather would make me feel I was a traitor to consider this. It was nearly nine years before I did a thing. At that time my sister had no interest. I suppose that because I had been with him when I was young I was more conscious of the relationship.

'In 1979, when I started to look for him, I toyed with the idea of talking to my mother but, although it was never a secret, I had never actually questioned her because I felt it was her personal life and had nothing to do with me. She didn't indicate ever that she knew where he was so I didn't feel she was the person I could approach. I didn't tell her what I was going to do.'

She did outline her situation to the Salvation Army but could not enclose any papers of proof because her mother, like 'Jenny's', had left them all in America. It was only from family conversations in her childhood that she was able to consider starting her search in Rochester, New York.

'The Salvation Army reminded me most frequently of certain things I hadn't considered like the fact that my father may have made a new life for himself with someone who had no knowledge of my existence and that I should consider whether I was ready to upset a stable family unit.'

This is a sensible piece of advice for anyone to bear in mind as they commence their search for a father.

'A year and a half passed with a periodic letter to say either that there was no progress or to ask for more information which I was unable to give. Then, finally, they wrote to inform me that they had located him. He was still in New York State and had agreed I could have his address in case I would like to write to him.

'After six attempts I wrote to this man whom I did not know how to address or what to say. In the end I started with his first name and went on to explain why I had waited so long to find him.

'I had a wonderful letter back. "Dear Cora-Ann," which was what I had been called in America, "You forgot to write your surname." You could sense the nervousness in the letter.

'From then on the correspondence flowed for more than a year. My father sent greetings from people who had known me as a child; they all said later that it was a prayer answered. He also said it was his dearest wish to see me and if I could consider coming, he would send the money for a ticket.

'It was a very emotional journey. I did more thinking on that plane than I'd ever done in my life before – not about what was going to be but how my mother was going to deal with the situation. Although, I knew I had to do it.'

Cora had to fly in to Toronto which was the closest airport to her father's home:

'It was horrendous. Two Jumbos had arrived simultaneously – nothing like I imagined. I didn't know where to start looking. There were ten thousand people meeting everybody – it was a snake of faces. I thought, no point in looking, just keep walking till the line peters out. Then I saw this very serious-looking, white-haired man standing in a corner. He said my name. I just burst into tears. Although he was my father, I wasn't looking at him as a father but when he said my name it triggered off all the emotion and we just sobbed.'

Her father had made provision for such an emotional reunion by bringing along a friend to act as chauffeur for what was a six-hour journey one way from his home.

'My father never let go of my hand. He told me he had waited twenty years before he married again and his wife was a younger woman close to me in age. She was very nervous at first but we got on well together. She had taken some holiday time from her job to be with me.'

Cora admits she fell totally in love with everything in the States. On her return home, her mother asked only if she had had a nice time. By then, for all her pleasure at being there, she had also been able to see what her mother must have been up against when she first arrived there:

'I realised she must have been out of her depth in what she saw as a alien culture. My father has a very dictatorial manner. I can relate to how she must have felt as a nineteen-year-old and possibly a bit hot-headed herself.'

While there, her father had asked for her sister's address. Cora suggested it would be better to give his to her. Her sister did decide to write to her father and then a year later flew over to meet him, but was not as enamoured of the States as Cora had been.

Cora has since returned several times and is seriously considering whether to live there. She, of course, would have no problem working there because she is an American by virtue of her parents' marriage and the fact that her father registered her with the appropriate authority when she was born.

In 1986, both sisters went over to a very special family occasion – a gigantic picnic:

'They were coming from all over the States to attend. It was to take place in a bay off Lake Ontario where my uncle owns a summer house. It was so organised that all along the highway were big notices saying "The Turchetti Picnic This Way" every ten miles. It was absolutely wonderful.'

Since then Cora has made the decision to live in America and is now there with her daughters.

Family gatherings such as the above play a big part in the reunions between fathers and their British children. As Bruce W. from Northamptonshire found, it seemed that everyone wanted to be in on the pleasure of meeting this new member of the family.

His mother had used the excuse of her pregnancy to go home to England: 'From a very early age I knew that my father was American although my mother never spoke about him.' Nor, it would seem, did she provide any explanation for the fact that every Christmas a parcel would arrive containing gifts:

'And always a bag of shelled pecan nuts. It was sent by my American grandma known as "Mama Henley". In later years I was to discover that my mother had regularly sent photographs of me to her and she displayed them in her lounge alongside those of her other grandchildren.'

In 1974, Bruce received a letter from J.T. Henley, a clerk to the circuit Judge in Desha County, Arkansas. 'He told me that he was my uncle and that his daughter and her husband, who was a Methodist minister, were coming to England to attend a church conference and he hoped we could meet.' It was from this cousin that Bruce learned a lot more of what had happened and that his father was the Sheriff in Eldorado, Arkansas – a far cry from his own life in Northamptonshire!

By this time, Bruce had a wife and small child and could not consider the cost of a visit to his father. Then, his paternal grandmother died and when the family gathered for the funeral, a decision was made to club together and send him $500 towards the fare.

When he flew in on 19th May, 1978, he was met by his cousin who had already visited him in England and the uncle who had set the reunion in motion.

> 'The next day, my cousin had a fish-fry party for us to meet the rest of the family. Odis [his father] wasn't expected to be there as he had to work, but when we arrived, his car was parked outside the house. We went in. There must have been thirty or forty people there; they all stopped talking and looked at me. My cousin took me over and introduced me to my father. I was thirty-two years old and meeting him for the first time. We shook hands and said "Hello"; we were both unsure and conscious of everyone watching, wondering what was going to happen. Nothing did; after all those years, it wasn't like a father and son meeting, it was just two men talking together. He told me that had he known at the time that my mother was pregnant, he would not have let her come back to England.'

What this GI had realised was that because his wife had never travelled more than a fifteen-mile radius from her home, America had seemed very strange to her. He was working long hours and she was lonely. He must have thought that a trip home would cure her of homesickness.

'He took several well-creased photographs of me as a baby out of his wallet.' It was obvious that circumstances, not lack of love, had kept this father and son apart.

This reunion with his father was to cause a breakdown in the good relationship Bruce had had with his stepfather but, as he says: 'It is strange that when one door closed with my mother's death and my stepfather severing all contact with me, another door opened in America.' To Bruce, America was no longer a distant land. To his mother's generation it was as remote as Siberia, which was why, as reality dawned, some were afraid to try living there in the first place. This left the GIs they married the choice of staying on with their wives in England or seeing an end to the marriage before it had even begun.

A few were willing to give married life in the UK a try. One father was fine until he heard that his family was setting up a lumber business back in Washington state: 'He was only supposed to go over to help them get started but he never came back.' In appealing to the Veterans' Administration for help, this daughter has received conditions which have not even been imposed on illegitimate children taking this route. In any communication she sends her father via them, 'I have been told I cannot put any personal identification on it or my address.' This seems ludicruous given that she has every legal right to try to reach her father. She is taking additional steps such as going through the local phone book – which is not quite as difficult as it seems because she knows that her father had five brothers. She has also decided to approach the leading paper in Seattle to see if they will do a feature on her search: 'My father came from such a big family, there must be one of them that knows about me.'

Regardless of the reasons for their parents' marriage breakdown, children where mothers returned home from America are less prone to blame themselves and are less likely to side with their mother's version of events. They will wish to make their own judgements. They will also see America through different eyes, not understanding why their mother made an instant turnaround, and definitely wanting to give their fathers the chance to explain themselves.

They might even be old enough and experienced enough to realise that Mum may have been too voluble too early in her criticism of her new home and too tiresomely homesick – not what the American 'mom' would have wanted in a daughter-in-law who therefore would have encouraged her back to Britain for a visit.

There is no doubt that many of these GI brides did not meet with the proudly American mom's approval. Nevertheless this humiliation was still better than the long silence suffered by some brides as they waited to be sent for and gradually realised they were never going to go.

David M. of Middlesex has the high cheekboned look of his American Indian ancestors who married into a pioneer German family who have been in Pennsylvania since the early nineteenth century. 'I think I knew from the start that my father was a GI and was always proud of it. I'd always thought about going to the States and meeting him.' The reason why his mother had never gone there was a subject which always brought tears. She may have missed being registered as a bona fide bride which would have qualified her for free passage. She had made one of the earliest marriages before the American Military authorities prepared for the rush of women who would have to be shipped to the States.

Once back in the States, and probably unaware of the free facility of transport, David's father found that he could not afford to send for them (by now he had two sons). Transatlantic travel was an expensive undertaking. As an example, one bride was too impatient to wait for free passage and persuaded her father to pay the air fare. It cost £100 which at that time was more than many British working men made in a year!

David's mother eventually divorced his father and later married again. He admits he resented the man 'because he wasn't my father and if a man was coming into the house, I wanted my American dad. I'd saved a Christmas card he'd sent me as a little 'un. It was my treasure.'

In his mid-teens he began to think about looking for his father because by then all contact had stopped. It took a lot of gentle persuasion to get his mother to hand over the last known address. He took this to the Red Cross to ask for help but they were unable to trace him. 'I tried writing to that last address but it was returned "unknown".'

He married young and the idea of finding his father was shelved while he started a family. But he never needed to pick up his clues again:

> 'I had a phone call. My uncle had asked friends in England to look me up in the book. My Aunt Jackie came on the line and asked me some questions then said, "Your uncle would like to speak to you." I can't remember who said what after that, I was in shock.'

It was revealed that the reason his uncle had taken the initiative was because his father was deaf and unable to use a telephone: 'I asked if my father wanted to see me or for me to write to him and received his address.' It turned out that this GI, like so many transient Americans, had moved and was now living 150 miles from his original town.

David sensibly wrote a 'this is me' kind of letter as a starter and by return learned that his father had married again and that he had seven more brothers and a sister.

'I decided from the day my uncle phoned, that I was going to the States and managed it the following year (1985).' His uncle met him and it would seem that there was an instant bonding; probably because this was the first contact he had made with the family. His uncle also took a proprietorial interest because he'd been the one who had actually found him. In addition, he had more space in his home and that was where David and his wife and children stayed. There were get togethers at various other family houses and through them David began to learn about his German heritage. He also found the outdoor life available was wonderful: 'I did lots of fishing; they are so big there that I have no interest in fishing now I'm home again.'

By virtue of where the family lived, he became immersed in American history: the Shenandoah Valley, the scenic Susquehana River and then – local pastimes. 'My dad didn't like it when my brother Woody and I beat him at horseshoes.' He found a natural affinity for this particular brother who was very much like him in appearance and interests.

The family cemetery was also fascinating. There were grave-stones from the Civil War and he discovered one about which the rest of the family knew nothing: 'It said "George Mixell, 1882" and next to it was another member of the family who had died in the Battle of Gettysburg.'

When he relayed all this exciting information to his British brother he found that there was no interest. Research is beginning to show that if there was more than one child left behind, it is usually the elder of the two who is most keen on claiming the American heritage.

'Cheryl' was another child of a GI who was faced with absolute silence from her mother which told her that the subject of a missing father was either too painful or embarrassing to discuss. The story of how she found him was picked up by the *Ladies Home Journal* in the UK and is worth repeating as an encouragement to others and as an illustration of the coincidences that can lead to the missing GI father.

'Cheryl' saw a news story on British television which featured an American reporter with the same last name as her father's. 'After five years of searching, I was willing to try anything so I wrote to him.' A month later, when she had given up hope of hearing from him, her telephone rang and it was the reporter to say that he had found her father. 'I didn't hear much after that; I was crying.' She was to discover that this young man had been so intrigued by her request that, while he was not related to her father, he was willing to plough through the 253 names in the directory which were also 'Roths'.

It was arranged that 'Cheryl's' father would telephone her. After their shared tears he was able to explain that he had not looked for her because he had thought she would not want to hear from him. She, for her part, had thought he was indifferent. Thus are misunderstandings built up out of all proportion.

Their actual meeting was organised by the *Pittsburgh Post Gazette*, British Airways and the Pittsburgh Hilton:

'When we finally arrived [her husband accompanied her] we were treated like celebrities. Television crews took our pictures and we were ushered to the head of the line in customs. Then I stepped on to an escalator and rose slowly to meet my father; a TV cameraman blocked my way but I peered round him and there was Dad coming towards me. As I rushed to meet him he was crying too hard to say anything. He just hugged me tight and patted my back again and again.'

By the end of that visit, 'Cheryl' and her husband had decided to up sticks and go and live close to her father who had by now retired to Florida. This is a rare ending to such a reunion; usually when the euphoria evaporates children see the sense of staying put.

This news came as a shock to her mother but she has had to accept that while it had been her choice not to live with her GI husband in America, the child of that marriage and the father are owed years to learn more about each other.

Someone else who has had to make up for lost time was thirty-eight before she discovered that the woman whom she had always believed to be her mother was in fact her grandmother. Whilst sorting through her late 'mother's' effects, she came across a wedding photograph of a GI and a young girl whom she then realised was her mother. She had died when she was born.

By then, her father had gone off as part of the invasion forces in France and her grandmother had been determined to hold on to the baby. 'She lied through love of me.'

After locating the church, this woman discovered the necessary details of her personal history which included the fact that her grandmother had destroyed all the letters that had come from her father as well as the visa he sent so that she could join him.

Determined to make amends for what had been done, she was fortunate to secure the help of a local man who had begun to make a hobby of finding GI fathers and through him located her father in North Carolina. He revealed that at first her grandmother had written to assure him that everything was fine. Then, when the letters stopped he assumed his child had chosen to stay with her grandmother and he went on with his life.

There has since been a grand family reunion which included the siblings from the father's second marriage.

Richard C. of Northumberland has been thwarted from enjoying such pleasure. This is a tragic end to the efforts of a 'friend' of TRACE who found the final clue to that father's whereabouts when he recognised the father's name in an obituary of Richard's grandmother. This led to a long telephone discussion between the 'friend' and the father. In spite of this, he is not responding to letters from his son.

Richard does not know what caused the marriage of his parents to break down, which is why he proposes to be patient:

'I have tried not to bombard him with letters. Indeed, I have only sent a handful since I was given his address. I want him to feel – and of course his new wife – that they are not being pressurised. My letters remain unanswered, but I vow I will never surrender the hope that one day my father and I can meet as friends and I will work ceaselessly to that end so long as we both live.'

It does seem rather sad that in such circumstances these fathers cannot unbend enough to spare a few kind words for children who have, through no fault of their own, been left out of their lives for so long. In talking to them, even giving way to one meeting, they could remove the usual first suspicion that anyone was after their money. Some have even found, to their surprise, that they can be taken care of by their children, if necessary.

In spite of a legitimate marriage to a GI, plus his name on the child's birth certificate, the question of genuine fatherhood still rears its head.

'Dale' was aware as he was growing up that he had a GI father. Even though he was an unknown figure, or perhaps because of this, 'Dale' admits to a fascination with things American. 'When cast lists came up on films or television, I always looked for his name. I wanted to see it written down. I realised that more than likely in America there were blood relations.'

His mother married again after her divorce and out of respect for his stepfather, he left the subject alone, happy with the man he called 'Dad'.

Then, at fourteen, rummaging through the assortment of photographs his grandmother kept in a shoe box, he came across one of a man in uniform and asked who he was. There was no more explanation other than this was 'a friend of the family'. When he pondered on this statement, having also been aware of the American uniform, he realised this must be his father.

'Dale' went back for a closer inspection and found that the photograph was missing. As children do, he sensed he should not ask why.

'Then, as I was growing older I felt that my natural father was too and that if I left it too late, I would never see him.

'Right at the beginning, the US Embassy practically slammed the door in my face and said there would be no chance. The British Red Cross were more helpful and suggested the American Red Cross. They put me on to the National Personnel Records Center in St Louis, who notified me that they had had a big fire which had destroyed the records I needed.'

'Dale' was to try the Salvation Army, War Babes, the Burtonwood Association (Burtonwood airfield in the north was allocated to the GIs in World War II), and the Governor of Iowa, who in turn directed him to the Veterans' Administration of that state who said that they had no one by that name on their files. Then he heard about TRACE who questioned why he had started his search in Iowa: 'I needed to find my roots, my ancestors, and my mother had told me this was my father's home state.'

His problems began when she changed her mind and suggested it might be Ohio. Since both states would have a similar sound to the unfamiliar ear, this was an acceptable mistake. However, some of her other information conflicted and 'Dale' began to wonder if she was deliberately trying to confuse him.

As he kept going, he worried that the blind alleys he encountered were eating into what he saw as his limited time factor. Nevertheless, he held on to the hope that if his father was dead, he might at least find some half-brothers or -sisters who would look like him since there was no matching resemblance with the siblings of his mother's second marriage.

After a while, Mum's 'recollections' began darting from Savannah, Georgia to California in a lightning dash across the States. His uncles who were teenagers at the time of the marriage began to correct some of the details she supplied. This was an age when if there had been any 'misbehaviour' by big sister who was married, they would have certainly been alert to the odd whisper between adults. Then, for some reason, they suddenly became uncooperative and insisted they had been confused. 'Dale' began to smell a whiff of collusion, compounded by the fact that his story had become more complicated when he discovered that his mother's marriage to the GI had run into difficulties at an early stage. The American had been arrested and charged with a serious crime and 'Dale's' dutiful mother seems to have become very friendly with one of the GI guards when she visited her husband in jail.

'Dale' faces a growing suspicion that this man may have been his father because, while trying to unravel the mystery, he has found this other man's name on his baptismal certificate: 'And my grandmother was such a strictly religious lady, I do not think she would have allowed a lie.'

However, was the name on that baptismal certificate perhaps the grandmother's way of protecting the child from being labelled the son of a criminal? He might never know, but he has discovered that when that guard at Burtonwood jail was transferred, he continued to write to his mother until after he was born.

'Dale's' only other clue to his identity is a memory that as a young man off to visit a girlfriend, he passed a woman who stared at him intently and then asked his name. She said he was the image of the GI his mother married.

'Dale's' true identity could rest on the date he was conceived. If it was before the GI husband was taken into custody, he must he his. He has yet to find how these important dates correlate.

Meanwhile, Mum can't or won't help.

One of the saddest stories relating to the child of married parents came to me via a telephone enquiry from Patrick who wanted help in finding a brother in Florida.

His parents were married and went to live in lodgings, quite a common occurrence then. It was planned that mother and baby would stay there until the GI dad could arrange for them to join him in Canton, Ohio. When neither money nor tickets came as promised, Patrick's mother thought she had been deserted and with no money to pay the rent, she was thrown out of her lodgings.

There was little help for anyone in such circumstances in those days and eventually she took up with someone who treated her badly, and the child worse. Patrick was beaten so viciously he has suffered from epilepsy ever since. His mother never gave up on finding her GI and before she died (at forty-six) she begged her son to keep up the search.

None of the agencies he contacted were able to help but, fortunately, he had not been forgotten by the family in the USA. A cousin visiting the UK went to St Catherine's House and found four possible names. Each received a letter.

'I will always remember the opening lines of my uncle's letter which said, if I bore any malice and did not wish to reply, they would understand. They did not know how long I had prayed for this day. I could not dial the telephone number, I was shaking so much and when I heard that voice at the other end, it was like somebody giving me a whole new world.'

But it was one that no longer held his father. Patrick was to learn that money and tickets had been sent to the lodgings where they had been appropriated by the landlady who wrote back without his mother's knowledge to inform his father that they would not be coming to the States. He then applied for a divorce and sent the papers. The landlady then forged the necessary signature of agreement and proceeded to pocket the allowance that was sent monthly for the child.

Fortunately, Patrick is now enjoying the happy ending for which he is long overdue. He has not only had a visit from some of his family but they have sent him tickets to visit them there.

'We had to split my holiday, staying with each of the family in turn. Some lived in Illinois, others in Canton, Ohio, where a big family reunion was planned for 4th August which was the Hall of Fame football parade weekend.

'My proudest moment came when over dinner one night, not long after we arrived, my uncle stood up and presented me with my father's Bible and a full American flag. I had never had anything in my life which belonged to my father and he had left this for me.

'Uncle Harold took us to the Courthouse to get my Dad's Army discharge papers and birth certificate. Since our return, my American family have sponsored me for my citizenship which I gained automatically through parentage. They are prepared to help us find a place and settle in.'

What makes this story worse is the fact that some of the relatives in England had discovered the landlady's deception but decided not to tell Patrick's mother. Understandably, he is furious but he is compensated in part by having a loving family in the United States who are trying to make up for lost time.

NINE

We Get By with a Lot of Help from Our 'Friends'

Someone who has already been praised by Jim K. for her help in reaching his black father in Alabama and who has also helped countless other members of TRACE – Transatlantic Children's Enterprise – would be seen by many of them as their best friend. Sophia Byrne began her work after reading about my involvement with TRACE in the *South Wales Argus*. Her original intention had been only to assist someone she knew. This was accomplished so fast and was so satisfactory that she volunteered to help anyone else who might need her. Very shortly after that Sophia became the membership secretary of the group.

Like me, she ends up offering much comfort and counselling as well as basic advice. Her only complaint is that she wishes more people would let her know after they reach that 'happy ending'. This is quite understandable, bearing in mind that like many of us she does this work voluntarily, and therefore those successes are like a reward.

People who join TRACE are advised how to use the information they already have, however minimal that might be. If they at least know the state, they are put in touch with a 'friend' if there is one residing there or nearby.

These 'friends' have built up in number over the years and allow TRACE members a personal contact – someone who knows the area and is often willing to make discreet enquiries on their behalf. In cases where the father has died, they have been able to obtain a death certificate which in turn can lead to next of kin, as has already been illustrated. A 'friend' alerted to the family name can keep an eye on obituary columns in the local paper.

Some of these 'friends' are able to ascertain which high school the GI attended and obtain from them copies of the appropriate year-book. This particular American custom is of great value to British children because it contains that elusive photograph. We have also had instances where they have been able to approach the alumni secretary of their father's college from whom they have received his current address.

Various circumstances have led to the collection of these 'friends'. The first were the ladies who had been part of my book *Sentimental Journey*. One of whom was Barbara in Oregon. Once she had discovered the GI was dead she found his sister and put her in touch with his child.

When *Sentimental Journey* became available in American libraries, readers who had links with the UK, and thought it evocative enough to write to me, found they had been automatically enlisted into the army of 'friends' of TRACE. None has as yet deserted.

I have also involved the American half of my family. When I was in the USA in November 1989 for a wedding, my cousin's husband Dudley chauffeured me around Washington to various Veterans' offices to investigate what services they could provide in finding missing fathers. He continued to chase up one promise made by an official until he was sent the very useful *Armed Forces Locater Directory* which will be discussed later.

Another cousin's husband, Willie, together with his wife, divides the year between London and New York. This means he is accessible for questions when he is in residence here and can follow things up when he returns to America. His claim to know every inch of New York City has proved invaluable to more than one person and he feels strongly that if he can help out, why not? He was able to send someone, whose father is dead, a detailed map of her father's neighbourhood including his primary school. But even he has been stumped by the one elusive thread in this story which was to find the Aunt Rose who had sent baby clothes to England for her brother's baby in the 1940s. One has to assume she is a married lady and has moved on, address unknown to the locals he has questioned.

Certain states exceed others in their number of missing fathers. This means we are grateful for the fact that there is often more than one 'friend' there. After all, there is a limitation on how much time anyone can give. Consideration must be given to their expenditure on mail, telephone calls and driving. They receive some help with postage, but their time and effort is given generously.

There are also friends like Edna and Willard who are now resident in London but can discuss aspects of past and contemporary life in Philadelphia. They also follow through with telephone check-ups when they are over there for the annual visit. And 'Buddy' Weiner, ex-New Yorker, now resident in Berkshire. He has proved invaluable in answering questions relating to GIs in the London area.

Because these 'friends' play such an important part in the searches, examples of how they became 'friends' and do their work belong in this book. There are those of them who prefer to stay anonymous and unreported. The rest have offered their stories in their own words, providing ideas and encouragement for people searching for their GI fathers.

Olive has retired to Florida; her feelings about her early days as a GI bride are reflected in her words and give an insight into the receptions which could have driven the faint-hearted bride back to Britain or discouraged them from making the final step regardless of the baby.

> 'I'd have been so pleased if someone had helped me, so grateful. At first, I blamed the GI but the more I hear, the more I blame the utter callousness of the Military. I also blame the snobbish American women feeling that anyone other than the "girl next door" wasn't good enough; and they had so little to be snobbish about. Indeed, mothers had such power in our day. Those of us who had the courage to fight back made it. The others fell by the wayside. Also, I do not say this in any superior manner, I am my brother's keeper; if he hurts, so do I. I find it easy to feel the pain and almost consuming *need* to find a lost father. Maybe because I have always felt so close to mine.

Betty in California is a GI bride who missed being in *Sentimental Journey* but who I met via the authors of another book about the same period which devoted a chapter to GI brides: *The Yanks Are Coming*, by John Frayn Turner and Edwin Hale (Baton Press, 1983). She was a participant in the GI brides reunion, the idea for which I had suggested to the Southampton Tourist Centre when I was there researching my first book. I arranged for Betty to meet Andra who was looking for her father in California. By then, they had exchanged a few letters:

'Andra's genuine sincerity, warmth and charm grabbed me instantly. She wanted nothing from this man – monetary or materialistic. Only to be acknowledged and accepted as his daughter. She had folders of countless pieces of correspondence; photographs, old and worn, had been saved lovingly by her mother. We talked about her feelings of desperation. Not knowing her father. Not being able to find him. Unable to make direct contact. I was truly touched by her frankness and the efforts she had made over the years. I was determined to help her on my return to California.

'I made my first telephone call on her behalf hoping to act as intermediary between her and her father and to give him my personal impression of her. But, no matter how much tact and diplomacy I used, this man [the same one who had told Andra to write, care of him] was in charge of the conversation, refusing my request to speak to her father. Was it a nursing home? Was this man his nurse? I checked through Directory Enquiries, the City Hall and utility companies [gas, electricity and water]. I drove the forty-odd miles to the address but was unable to receive a response. I went back again and again, even asking neighbours if he lived there. Nobody knew anything!'

As we know, this man's solicitors have closed the case and Betty's help has been restricted by her husband's poor health.

As collaborator on *Sentimental Journey*, Brenda has had an extra special interest and is well aware of the scene with the girls as the GIs flooded into the Liverpool area. Anyone who applies to join TRACE from there is directed to her. She has built up a file of useful contacts which stretch beyond her home state of Arizona. In 1990, she had a flood in her house which left her in a panic because certain papers from members of TRACE were waterlogged. She dried as much as she could and an alert went out to members for anyone who had been in touch with her to repeat their details:

'I didn't quite know what I was getting into when my friend of many years, Pamela Winfield, said she was going to use me as a "friend" of her organisation. I did not know it would lead to a wonderful friendship with a young woman from Liverpool [Julia G.].'

Brenda has literally mothered Julia and compiled a file on her father who died five months before he was traced. She is currently trying to help her find one of her three half-sisters who might be more forthcoming than the one she has so far discovered.

'I have had harsh words from another woman who thought she was the only person I had to work with.' Fortunately, it is the rare member who takes advantage or is unappreciative of all the effort. This was one who did not recognise in the report of the failure to get past the widow to find another member of her father's family that it had been preceded by a lot of work, not only from Brenda but also from two other 'friends'.

'I have had gifts which are greatly treasured, but not really necessary, from people who have written to ask for help in locating part of their American family. The work is exhausting, exasperating, rewarding and depressing. All of those feelings enter into a search.

'Some people have a great deal of information but one young man, a German, was told nothing by his mother (now deceased). He is looking for his American father who had a "scar on his forehead, came from Texas and was called Bob". He begged that I would put his letter in a public place where many people pass! With the best intentions in the world, I am afraid this is an impossibility. All we can do, the network of "friends" Pamela has thrown across the United States like a spider-web, is to keep on hunting and hoping. Sometimes we wait and wait for answers while the person in England climbs walls wondering what we are doing. Sometimes, we don't get any answers at

all which is as exasperating for the searcher as for the looker.
We just have to keep on with the letter writing until something
turns up.'

The widespread effect of Brenda's efforts showed itself in late
1990 when a letter arrived from Stafford (UK). She had put an
ad about TRACE in a US magazine called *Searchers*. This was
seen by someone in Columbus, Ohio, who had a pen-friend in
the UK looking for a GI father!

Joan discovered a copy of *Sentimental Journey* in the Cleveland
library. She enjoyed it so much that she wrote a letter which
began a lively correspondence between us which was to lead to
her becoming a 'friend' of TRACE:

'I think I just fell into it. You wrote and told me about it. I
found it interesting, and when you sent a name of someone
in Cleveland and would I please look in the phone book – an
an accommodating person and because I have access to three
good libraries and old records – I started looking. [No luck –
we recently found he had died in 1961 and didn't come from
Cleveland anyway, he came from a town 150 miles southeast
called Steubenville].'

This is an example of the problems that are constantly
encountered. The GI often gave the girl the name of the closest
town of any merit rather than admit to coming from a small or
little-known place.

Joan followed up this discovery by sending to the Chamber of
Commerce for some information about Steubenville which led to
a British child discovering that she had a link with the pioneering
days of America. Steubenville, perched on the Ohio river, was part
of the nineteenth-century covered wagon push into the Western
Territories. There were twenty-five similar names in the phone
book which Joan has now sent to this TRACE member who will
try to find a relative.

'You sent me other names and I obliged – I guess you might
say I lived through the era of World War II and understand the

circumstances of some of the "conceptions"! After the war, I worked with pregnant ex-servicewomen at the Soldiers', Sailors' and Airmen's Families Association (SSAFA), heard their stories, and found myself wondering what would happen to them and their babies. I only remember one mother-to-be who said she would keep her baby; the rest were going up for adoption. So I sort of had a sympathetic background, you might say.'

In this capacity, Joan tries very hard. One of the people she has helped had an address for her father, but a detective agency had told her that it did not exist. At the point where Joan stepped in, the woman had already placed an ad in a service publication and had received a response from a friend of the GI, giving a PO box number in Ohio.

Having a PO box number assures a person of privacy and only a court order can break into the system. One can, of course, get round this by hiring a private detective to watch who opens the box and follow them, but it is a very expensive undertaking.

'So, having the man's PO box address, they [the woman and her husband] sent a letter to him saying she wanted to know whether or not he would acknowledge her. He did not reply but as the letter was not returned, it must have been received. Then they put an ad in the local paper and this is where I saw it and had a hunch they might be looking for a father. I wrote to them and told them about TRACE and so we began another long saga.

'I searched local phone books, and followed up the original street address in street directories and city directories for many hours at four libraries and passed on all the names and addresses. They telephoned every name without success. Some of them were obviously related; two or three in the same house as the father. Now they slam the phone down. They also engaged a lawyer to write a letter to the PO box in which they asked the man to contact the lawyer as he had some information to impart.

'It was never their intention to intrude on his life. She wanted her father to acknowledge her and, if at all possible, for them to get to know one another. However, always silence. The letter sent by the lawyer was returned, not accepted by the

131

GI. They think someone else might be picking up the mail and trying to shield him from an "unwanted" intruder so they keep persevering. I would like to see a conclusion to this case, it is getting under my skin.'

The problem was still irritating her a year later so when she was in the reference room of a library on another errand, Joan could not resist consulting the newest Dickman *Criss Cross Directory* for 1991.

'I flipped through the Oakdale streets [the original address she had been given], remembering that I had scanned them thoroughly a year or more ago, and once again looked down the lists of tiny print. The GI's name hit me between the eyes, only it was Oakwood, not Oakdale, a two-family house as there were two separate names for the house.

'This was a major find. Of course, it is not an open and shut case, it just means I have located where the man lives after four years of scrutiny – and bear in mind there was a four-inch file on it before I came on the scene. Quite incredible!'

Frustratingly for Joan and with apologies to the reader, the GI's daughter in England was on holiday when she tried to reach her so we have yet to know how she will deal with this information or if the GI will now respond.

'Friends' of TRACE start out with the attitude 'I'll give it a try' then find they cannot help but get more and more involved.

Jean in Wisconsin began that way by checking on the divorce papers for a TRACE member because she was fascinated by genealogy. Her most recent coup on the members' behalf was the result of intelligence from another 'friend' who notified me that there would be a reunion in Wisconsin of some of the men who had served in the USAF in Essex. On her next visit to England, Jean was able to hand me a copy of their roster. This was passed to Sophia who will make one of her eagle-eyed searches in the hope that some of those names will match the TRACE list of missing fathers.

Phyllis, another ex-Londoner, was drawn in on a visit to England:

'When I first met Pamela Winfield in 1988, I had heard a little about TRACE from the friend I had travelled with who had been helping for some time. [This was Sonia, who I nobbled at the GI brides reunion in Southampton and who has connections in Florida and Tennessee.] At that stage I didn't really know how it worked but Pam wasted no time in telling me about the organisation, and how it operates with the help of "friends". I was fascinated with the amount of work that goes on on a voluntary basis. The whole concept of TRACE spurred me into becoming involved.

'At present, I am in contact with several GI children and I am trying to help them. It isn't an easy task as so many years have passed and people in this country tend to move around a lot and don't stay in their home towns as we do in the UK, but we do the best we can with the information we have which is sometimes quite meagre. We rejoice when there are successes, and mourn with our GI children when there is bad news. Some of them are in touch with us quite often and we become friends in the true sense of the word; others don't and we wonder if our leads have been successful. But we keep on trying to help. That's what "friends" are for.'

Lyn in Iowa is a comparative newcomer on the scene and delighted to make contact with people from Wales, the home she left to go to America but which she still loves dearly.

'I became a "friend" of TRACE purely by accident. I read an article by Pamela Winfield about a Scottish war bride. [Her late husband's family had come from Scotland.] I'm an avid letter writer so I wrote to Pamela, then received a letter from a lady in Cardiff asking me if I could trace her husband's father. [I don't always ask first – I just tempt them with a letter from "home".]

'It is my belief that every child should know who his or her natural parents are. Some of the GIs were never aware of the fact that they had fathered children (either in or out of wedlock). These men are, for the most part, glad to know of the child's existence and quite often parent and child have been reunited with benefits on both sides. I was well loved as a child and I wrote stories about my Welsh childhood.

'In the past, the difficulty in tracing the GIs was because of the US Invasion of Privacy law which made information extremely hard to get. However, as of late 1990 this situation was modified.

'I too have benefited from TRACE as I now have a new Scottish friend in Oregon and some in England and Wales. I would urge everyone to help as it is a worthwhile organisation and I am proud to be a "friend". We all need to belong to a family and I will do my best to make this come about.'

Much to Lyn's delight late in May 1991, she was to be visited by Lorraine E. from Malvern who she had been helping because her father's last known address turned out to be in Iowa. Lorraine's father was dead; she had missed seeing her half-sister, who had also died, by a few months, but will be meeting an aunt and uncle and visiting areas in Iowa with Lyn.

Lest the reader think that females dominate our list of 'friends', let me quickly bring in Harold Ludwig's point of view:

'I was nineteen, an American GI from a small town east of St Louis when I sailed in to Liverpool. For the next thirty months I would put my training and skills to work at Stoke-on-Trent, Staffordshire, where a chemical lab was set up at the Blythe Colour Works in the small community of Cresswell.

'I was one of the lucky ones, I guess, only a buzz bomb or two in London and some enemy bombings plus a couple of flights into Germany on a B-24 as an incendiary expert put me in touch with the real war. I think my obituary would have been just a line or two except that beside me there is now a filing cabinet with 417 letters from GIs' sons and daughters who were born in the UK during World War II or shortly afterwards. These have all been received since 1985 after a trip to England on vacation with my youngest daughter.

'During that stay my life took a change. I didn't know it at the time but thereafter I would spend hundreds of hours pursuing those GI fathers who had faded into the heterogeneous landscape of the United States after the war.

'I had written a letter before the trip to the Grand Hotel in Stafford and asked them to put a little notice on the bulletin board that said I was seeking a meeting with a girl I had dated late in 1943 but who had dumped me when I double-dated a friend who had two girls and wanted me to escort one of them.'

This story was picked up by the national press where I saw it and offered an exchange of me helping him find the girlfriend for his help with what I was doing.

Harold's story also attracted the attention of the children of the GIs who saw him as a contact with the US. One of them was a man from Stafford whose father was stationed with the same unit as his.

'The management of the Blythe Colour Works have been very generous in letting us use the private club and even chairing the first large meeting in 1989.

'Of the 3,000 GIs in Camp Cresswell, I'm the only one to return and make himself known. My hours now spent trying to help find fathers is rewarding. It is, in a small way, something of a return for all that was given to me so many times while in the UK. Letters would come two or three a week after I returned to St Louis, even some from Australia. Some of the GI fathers were easy to find; some required much searching. A large percentage will never be found because of almost zero firm, solid, basic information.'

Harold has found, as we do in TRACE, that there is a suspicion that some mothers conveniently 'can't remember'.

'I have often been asked to put an article in the personal column of our St Louis *Post Despatch* newspaper. I have only seen this help in one case where a daughter was lucky enough to get her request in the "Martha Carr" column. [This was Wendy F., already mentioned in "Just a Photograph".]

'There are 200 cities in the US with a population of over 200,000 people; the number of newspapers is staggering. The reason the above case worked is because that column is syndicated and is published in many newspapers.

'Recent developments in the Justice Department have supposedly opened the door to information on GI fathers. [Harold's comments are based on the many searches he has made on behalf of GI children. Living in St Louis, he is well acquainted with the procedures of the National Personnel Records Center.] This has done very little to help those with sketchy information. If you have his Army serial number or whatever service he was in, he could generally be found before, anyway. If you have his old address, that's a winner sometimes, especially if it was a small town where everybody knew each other. None of the services keeps up-to-date addresses but if the GI had been in a Veterans' Administration hospital they might have his address; they are extremely tight-lipped, but will forward letters.

'One of the most frequent comments I get in letters is that the National Personnel Records Center here in St Louis when asked for info often say those particular records were destroyed in a fire – and they don't believe it. But, believe me, *I watched six blocks of buildings burn totally out of control.*

'In 1987, I read that Pam Winfield had written a book about the GI brides. I found it in our local library, enjoyed it immensely and through sources in England found her address. We met in London in 1989 and now she refers people to me from around the St Louis area. One of them gave me a street name in St Louis as Burlington Junction. If you are a local that immediately sounds like a non-existent street name. Of course, I looked it up on the metro maps. No such name or even close to it. I deduced it could be a city or town in Missouri. Sure enough, there was a Burlington Junction in the north-west part of the state. I tried the name given to me. The operator said no one by that name lived there. I decided to ask for the mayor's office.

'A nice, elderly lady answered and I told her my story. "Why,

I went to high school with him and know his family well," was her reply and she got me the name of a cousin and from there, case closed or almost.

'We located aunts, uncles, cousins – all anxious to meet their English relative. All knew of her birth. Her father had disappeared because at the end of the war a letter arrived for him from England from this daughter's mother saying that she was packing up and coming to the US [she never did]. Old GI Joe has yet to be found though I think he will. His daughter plans a trip in 1991 and will get a great reception.

'So, I continue to receive letters; I write letters; I make phone calls; I bug the National Personnel Records Center, my American Legion service officer, and call many GI fathers and break the news. I have only had one bad experience in tackling the GI father. I hear he is big, bad and mean. Thank goodness many miles separate us – and in three years, he hasn't busted down the front door yet.

'Numerous American wives of these GIs have called me a few names at first, but afterwards have written to say that the English girl or man was the nicest of people they ever met in their lives. Most Americans and Brits get along great even if there is a "War Babe" involved.

'I am now retired and as I approach my 67th birthday, I wouldn't change a thing if I had to do it all over again.'

Harold harbours happy memories of his time in the UK and, like many GIs, makes frequent visits to where he was stationed. When I see such arrivals announced in the press I am ready to pounce.

Allen Petersen, who was on General Eisenhower's SHAEF staff (Supreme Headquarters Allied Expeditionary Forces) stationed at Bushy Park, England, was initially bribed to help by me sending a copy of *Sentimental Journey* for his British wife. He is now a 'friend' of TRACE and I am a 'friend' of SHAEF. This means we exchange newsletters. I must confess that theirs go on to Sophia Byrne who combs them carefully, always alert to the fact that she might just find a match to one of our missing fathers.

Allen has also been willing to brave some wives in the US on behalf of their husbands' British children. In one case, he tried the 'old buddy' routine to reach the one whose mother had ruined the original telephone contact the daughter made. A hostile lady refused to budge from the doorstep or let him talk to the man and that case has to be written off. In a similar situation, where he did manage to speak to the GI, the man denied all knowledge of what had happened in England. However, as Allen points out, the wife stayed in the room so he may have been practising the art of self-preservation.

We have gained 'friends' from other sources. Ann R., who found her father in the last few days she was in America, learned of a publication called *The Good Sam Club* which goes out to people who travel around the country in their mobile homes. She placed an ad in there, asking for help. This resulted in several volunteers.

After Ann's search ended, some were willing to become 'friends' of TRACE, like the man who was responsible for noticing Richard C.'s grandmother's obituary notice and made a long, emotional call to the father on behalf of his son. He has declined to make any observations for this book, but should he read it, I hope he realises he is truly thanked.

Virginia Holden in Pennsylvania has been equally kind. She is one of those ladies who lead an unbelievably busy and helpful life. She is a Gold Star Sister (which means she lost a brother in the war. He was with General Patton's Army and killed in December 1944). 'I would have swum over to bring his body back for burial here, but his wish was to be buried with his "boys".' She may feel that in reuniting these British children with their American fathers, she is doing a little something extra for one of those 'boys' who may have left a child in the UK.

Her interest in TRACE began after noting in her husband's *8th Air Force News*, that Ann R. was seeking information about her father who had been a prisoner of war in Germany during World War II.

'Any mention of a German PoW sends me to my copy of *Barbed Wire Interlude*, the story of Robert Ludden's (who was later a colleague at work) ten months' internment in Stalag IV. There are seventy-seven pages, forty-four of which list the names and home addresses of those he was able to contact. Through this, Ann found her father in Baltimore.'

Virginia also searches telephone books and has found that the regional office of the Veterans' Administration has been helpful in the past but is now referring enquiries on to the Department of Veterans' Affairs in Washington DC. 'The American Legion's headquarters in Harrisburg search their computer for names and this has been helpful in a couple of instances.'

What is even more important is the fact that Virginia knows some of these officials on a personal level. This extends to auxiliary friends in the Erie (Pennsylvania) area and her husband's cousin in Florida.

Her interest in this work becomes clearer when she writes that:

'Since meeting my husband in the Legion home in Manor in September 1949, my life has revolved around veterans: sewing, entertaining and cheering them up. I guess I sympathise with the men and women needing to know their biological fathers and want to help where I can. I enjoy hearing from all my contacts who have been most appreciative of anything done for them.'

Another Virginia who is a 'friend' was a personal friend of mine when she lived in London in the early 1980s. When she went to Texas I immediately enlisted her aid for TRACE. She was the one involved in the intensive search for the black father who was the son of a dentist who was supposed to have studied at a college in the Houston area.

She has since returned to live in the UK but still acts for TRACE, calling on her children in the States when the need arises. This led to her son acting as intermediary for Robbie W. with the series of telephone calls which finally got past the answering machine. She offers the following reasons for becoming a 'friend':

'Three weeks before I was born, my mother went to Abbie who had worked for her family since he was eleven years old and asked him to live with her and my father. He was in his sixties then and, as a second cousin of my great-grandmother, would tell me stories about my family and the town I grew up in that he remembered as a boy.

'Then there was my grandfather who, because he lived with my father's sister only a few blocks away, was a frequent companion with Abbie as we took our daily walks. Through him another slice of life about my family was portrayed. A totally different one for he was the son of a young army officer who had deserted the Kaiser's army and come to America a hundred years after my mother's family.

'I think of those two old men whenever I'm asked if I am being fair to a man's present family when they learn that their father, son or brother had a child from an affair while serving in the military. Oh, everyone agrees, it must have been difficult for someone to grow up without a father, especially in the day and age when "bastard" was as dirty a word as "whore". Still, isn't it better to let bygones be bygones rather than destroy the image of who he is today?

'Yet, as that is said to me, I remember those voices on the phone who have asked for TRACE's help in finding their fathers and, as I listen to their stories, I hear those two old men. They did not leave me money, fine paintings, or priceless antiques, but the knowledge of my heritage – a knowledge that helps me know who I am and where I'm from.

'Seeking that knowledge is why most men and women come to TRACE; they want to complete the person they are and will be. They want and need the heritage that most of us have always taken for granted. It's why I help and have my family help. Just as simple as that.'

TRACE gained another 'friend' through the efforts of Susan C. in 'Just a Photograph' who thought she had found her father but who alas was disappointed. Bud Maharian was very sympathetic to the situation because he too had been adopted as a child and had set out to find his blood parents:

'I actually met my mother and spent a weekend with her about two years before she died. I also met my father but it was decided between my sister [on that side] and I that we would not tell him who I was for fear that the shock would be too

WE GET BY WITH A LOT OF HELP FROM OUR 'FRIENDS'

great. We now suspect that he might have known that I was his son but we will never know because he also has died. My sister and I are alike enough to be twins.'

The most recent 'friend' is Philip Grinton who happened to be in the UK on holiday in March 1990 when the *Sunday Express* ran a story on the medical reasons why these missing fathers needed to be found. He telephoned and offered to help and came round to see me. As a retired Lieutenant Colonel with the US Corps of Engineers, he is a very methodical man who blanched when shown the cut-up pieces of cardboard on which I keep my records. (Thus do we keep the expenses of running TRACE down to a minimum.)

Those tacky cards did not deter him from his offer to assist which he sees partly as an extension of his interest in genealogy. He has already located some fathers and is very involved with letters to those seeking his help. This has not prevented him from keeping an eye out for any other means of improving on the searches and has recently discovered The Veterans' Alumni Association which will be discussed in the next chapter.

Someone who came to us via his own book was Lee Kennett, author of *GI*, published in 1987 in the US by Charles Scribner's Sons. A paperback edition by Warner Books is also available there. Lee had a year's sabbatical from being a 'friend' because he was at the Smithsonian in Washington, but he is now back with us as well as being at the Department of History in the University of Georgia.

As the successes continue, the group of 'friends' widens to include American relations of members. Helen P., who went over to surprise her father courtesy of his wife at their anniversary party, met a half-brother who lives in Chicago who offered to help. He has already been on a dangerous drive through a seedy section of Chicago to discover the address he had been given had long been vacated by that father. The search continues.

Elaine H. who appeared in 'Just a Photograph' has a sister who is poised to begin.

'For twenty-eight years I knew I had a sister in England but had no name to use to search, nor did I know how to start. It seemed like an impossible task. Everyone discouraged me when I would mention my desire to find her.

'When I discovered that a genetic syndrome in my family came from my father's X chromosome and all his daughters were carriers, I felt a desperate need to let my English sister know.

'TRACE helped my sister find me. I am willing to help American families learn about TRACE. There are probably many others wanting to find their English family members but who don't know about the organisation. I believe everyone has the right to know their families. We were so fortunate that Elaine and her family are precious, honest people. We truly love her.'

This chapter goes some way towards showing what an invaluable service 'friends' of TRACE provide. Although it can be an arduous task, they have all shown a willingness to keep going. All the hard work becomes worthwhile when they succeed in uniting a family.

TEN

How It Can Be Done

Having learned some of the procedures under which 'friends' operate, the time has come to take the process through from the discovery that 'my father was a GI'.

Everything that appears in block capitals will have the full address listed at the end of the book. More will be added because, as the book is being written, more useful organisations are appearing.

I must emphasise that none of this advice is meant to be professional. It has been collated on a strictly amateur basis over the years in which I have been involved in the work. Some derives from my personal knowledge of American life or from Sophia Byrne's breakdown of information that we have acquired through publications and newspaper cuttings sent to me from America.

While I was working on this book, the War Babes action against the US Department of Defence proved successful. Reports coming in so far from the initial few I have asked to be guinea pigs are mixed. It must be borne in mind that some will receive information that is forty years old. However, we are discovering the peripatetic American is going home to retire and 'home' is often that forty-year-old address.

What follows may be useful to those who at least have a name, coupled with a town or state. As has already been seen, the name that has a foreign flavour is a clue in itself, though it may involve a longer search to establish the home town or state. One cannot emphasise enough that the search is likely to be a long plod of letter writing.

As the book nears completion, TRACE continues to receive an average of three enquiries a week. This shows how deeply certain skeletons have been buried in the family closet. Initial requests to TRACE are responded to with an application form – one sheet of paper asking pertinent questions which will start them off on their search.

Because this group is recommended by the US Embassy and so many authoritative outlets, too many people are disappointed because they have assumed it is a high-powered agency willing to do all the work. However, the application form clearly states that the membership fee to TRACE covers administration costs, and that they are joining a self-help group.

Sophia Byrne, the membership secretary, worries over those who fall by the wayside so early, especially if they have already indicated they have the GI's service number because that is the key to their father's door. My feelings are that if they are not willing to fill in that form, they are not serious enough to stay the long and laborious course.

When starting, the most important piece of information which is often overlooked is their own date and place of birth. If, for instance, it was prior to the invasion of France, one may have to consider that the father did not return because he was killed in battle. The first thing to do is check if he was buried in one of the AMERICAN CEMETERIES in the UK or Europe. There, he may be easier to find without a service number. The CASUALTY AND MEMORIAL AFFAIRS DIRECTORATE in Alexandria, Virginia, does require a service number. The only exception is if the GI has an extremely unusual surname.

The place of birth could also be where Mum met Dad. If Mum retreated into anonymity because she was proposing to have her child adopted, there could be information in the archives of the home that she stayed in. There are several different adoption agencies which the CENTRAL REGISTRAR can supply. There is also the ARIEL BRUCE AGENCY in London (featured in a *Cutting Edge* documentary in spring 1991) which specialises in finding wartime mothers who were forced into the adoption decision.

As has been shown, the baptismal certificate can be useful (or a nasty surprise). If it is missing, a tour of the churches in the area might reveal the one that has it on file. However, several case histories have demonstrated that the name can be incorrectly spelled and variations may be necessary to reach the right one. Alternating an 'e' with an 'i' can make all the difference.

If the nationality appears recognisable, seek help either at the embassy of that country or a reference library where they will advise on the appropriate book to consult.

Not everyone is lucky enough to start with a full name. Mum may of course be prevaricating because she won't admit that she can't remember. I have to exercise an enormous amount of tact over this issue. No one likes to think that their conception was based on a brief encounter, but a large number were.

Newspaper archives in the town where the mother met the GI could have the necessary information on which military groups were there at the time. The PUBLIC RECORDS OFFICE at Kew has an enormous amount of logistical information but has to be visited in person, so does the US ARMY MILITARY INSTITUTE (Pennsylvania).

Some units have formed associations, with newsletters such as the BURTONWOOD TIMES and SHAEF COMMUNIQUE. The 82ND AIRBORNE have the STATIC LINE and the 82ND AIRBORNE DIVISION ASSOCIATION. THE NAVY TIMES, THE ARMY TIMES and THE AIR FORCE TIMES all have a locater column which allows one free entry. This method has produced quite a few fathers either by them seeing their names or friends recognising the clues and providing missing details.

While there was a preponderance of the US Army and Air Force in the UK, there are also addresses available for the US MARINES (RET) and MERCHANT MARINES which, it should be noted, is a separate entity.

Once one finds the headquarters of certain sections such as the US ARMY ENGINEERS at FORT LEONARDWOOD and the 8TH AIR FORCE HISTORICAL SOCIETY, they can also be approached. Special mention must be made of VIRGIL THOMPSON who is a great help with men who were in the USAF.

It has already been shown how, if the mother is dead, an advertisement in the local paper can bring forward people who knew her. Someone might remember the GI and supply that final tiny detail, even a nickname which will fill a missing space. 'Tex' is almost guaranteed to have come from Texas; 'Cookie' more than likely worked in a mess hall. If it is as unusual a name as 'Rooster', someone somewhere might remember why. One could surmise he was a man who rose at dawn or came from a farm – but from which state? Reference books in libraries would indicate the agricultural areas.

A full name that clearly indicates nationality could lead to starting in certain cities in the USA which are known to have large ethnic groups. If they have names which are part of American history, like Custer or Jefferson, a genealogical society can help. A good one to start with is THE NEW YORK GENEALOGICAL AND BIBLIOGRAPHICAL SOCIETY.

These societies are growing in number and take in early settlers' history as well as the more nationally known heroes. Names like Jefferson and Lee categorise them as southerners and in that generation would more likely have come from below the Mason Dixon line which cuts down the number of possible states.

Italian names suggest that it might be worth trying the ITALIAN AMERICAN WAR VETERANS. There are also separate associations for MEXICAN VETERANS and BLACK VETERANS and JEWISH VETERANS.

If one has the full name and service number, the usual official first stop has been the NATIONAL RECORDS CENTER in ST LOUIS. One has to remember Harold Ludwig's eye-witness account of the fire that destroyed a large number of records. Recently, however, copies have been found and anyone who has been notified by St Louis that their father's records were burned, should try again. It must be borne in mind that these records can be as much as forty years old, nonetheless it is information that could prove to be invaluable to a search. With it one can contact the VETERANS' ADMINISTRATION OFFICE in Washington DC, who will forward the enquiry to the appropriate place and, if requested, include a letter for the veteran. It is then up to him to reply. Bear in mind he may have moved several times since that address went on file, so it should not be seen as the final act in trying to reach him.

To the above can now be added the VETERANS' ALUMNI

ASSOCIATION discovered for TRACE by Philip Grinton. It aims to become a central post office for all veterans and, for a modest fee, will enable them to find each other. There are already several hundred thousand names and addresses on the list, but like the Veterans' Administration, will only forward letters and leave it to the recipient to reply.

With the GI's service number but no address, there are still a few short cuts possible. Sophia Byrne holds a code book, courtesy of a 'friend', which narrows down that number to a possible three states where he enlisted. While it has already been shown that, due to a job elsewhere, that may not have been his home state, it is worth the triple try.

There is a Veterans' Administration office at each state capital. The US Embassy will supply the list. There is also a Chamber of Commerce in each state capital and in most towns of any size. They will supply information about the father's home area and some have not been averse to sending copies of pages from the phone book listing the necessary name.

If the Veterans' Administration office in the state capital ignores the letter (give them six weeks), write to the Governor. He seems to have the ability to get them moving. Your reference library should have lists of US state capitals and if their address is not followed by the Zip code, you must get it, either from a post office or from Sophia Byrne at TRACE. Failing that, address the letter to the postmaster of the town and ask him to redirect it.

Probably the most useful source in the state capital is the Vehicle Licensing Bureau. This has proved to be the most reliable place to get a father's current address. Send them the name and approximate date of birth or age. Be warned that if it is a common name they could come back with several to choose from. Most important to remember is that like many of the other agencies, they will not reply unless sent the courtesy of an International Reply Coupon which can be purchased at any main post office.

Without knowing the specific state, one can either write individually to all fifty Vehicle Licensing Bureaux or to an agency like VEHICLE OPERATOR SEARCHES which specialises in this work. Their fee of $10 per state is probably only a good investment if the name is unusual.

If one has the GI's name and home town, he could be as close as a telephone call if International Enquiries provide a number. With this number comes the great decision – how to use it? It assumes great emotional proportions; it makes the father real – no longer just a name. At this point, panic can set in. Fear of rejection flares. Care should be taken in what one does next.

A lot depends on if the GI is aware he left a child behind. He may not have told his current family. This then would have some bearing on his reaction. He could be too shocked to respond favourably at once if he did not know he had left his British girlfriend pregnant. It may be necessary to say a few code words such as names of places before plunging in with the revelation of being his child.

The preferable, if slower way, once it has been established where he is, is to get his address and send a 'this is me' letter. As has been suggested, it should start with an apology in case it is truly a case of mistaken identity.

Knowing he has a phone number means he is in a directory. The larger, main libraries hold them and HOLBORN REFERENCE LIBRARY will send details if they are sent a stamped addressed envelope and note of explanation that you know he is in the book. This only holds if his number is not 'unlisted', but that at least establishes he is in residence in that town. Therefore, his address, if he drives, will be available via the Vehicle Licensing Bureau.

Any place that has a large selection of US phone books is worth a stop if one only has a name, because a random search could prove beneficial. Any match found can be written to in the guise of a 'researcher' into family history.

'Cousin clubs', Scottish clans and thriving genealogical societies are all happy to help. There is a far greater interest in ethnic roots now than there was twenty years ago.

One must be prepared to 'stretch' the truth in order to be successful. It is not so much lying as protecting the person to whom one is writing. More 'points' can be gained by allowing a way out. If I seem to be emphasising this too much, it is because *one could do so much damage to an innocent family with false accusations..*

Several people have indicated that they feel so uncomfortable 'telling lies', that they find it difficult to write a convincing letter even at the start when it is only to a Veterans' Administration official. But they should realise that revealing all could throw up a protective 'male preservation' barrier based on the 'this could be me' syndrome – bound to invalidate any help. 'Looking for a friend of the family' is no actual lie nor is it a misrepresenation to be 'researching' family history. It just makes for a better start.

Sophia Byrne and I each hold two directories which have proved invaluable. One is the *1989 Directory of Veterans' Service Organisation*; the other, *How to Locate Anyone Who Is or Has Been in the Military (Armed Forces Locater Directory)* by Lieutenant Colonel Richard S. Johnson. With these, depending on how much is known about the GI, we have been able to give more advice. For instance, if he won a Purple Heart he could belong to the MILITARY ORDER OF THE PURPLE HEART INC USA.

Mother should be encouraged to remember all the details of the 'getting to know you' conversations she may have enjoyed. If it included his high school or college, this is a great help. Remember that those high schools have that year-book which lists students with photographs.

The Alumni List of American colleges are in public domain and must, therefore, provide the last known address. The GI bill allowed returning servicemen to go to college free and many took advantage of this. There could be a clue in what he told Mum he hoped to do after the war was over.

If she can remember any other chat which relates to a family business or profession, he could be listed in the yellow pages of his home town.

If you are embarking on a search for a GI father you may well have taken notes whilst reading through this book. You will now also benefit from the personal accounts which follow. And if you have someone who is debating whether or not the search is worth it, the following might encourage them to have a go.

This is the reaction of someone who prefers to be nameless: 'I never dreamed I would be so wanted.' She found her father after a lot of disappointment but eventually when she wrote to the Drivers' Licence Bureau in Sacramento:

'Some nice person sent the address with no questions asked. I got in touch with the fire brigade at the place given. They hadn't enough men on duty for anyone to go out and investigate so they put me in touch with the police who went out for me. He had moved from that address and they spoke to the person who lived next door. I rang her and she gave me his new address. Perhaps the way I did it could help other members.'

We have discovered that the Vehicle Licensing Bureaux carry different titles and vary state by state. Some charge a fee, rarely very much; others respond by return of post; a few are now refusing. It may be as simple as the attitude of the clerk on duty when the request comes in, because most recently, Sacramento turned someone down.

The fact that 'Paul' is a doctor of science shows in his concise report which follows. He admits he saw the search as enjoyable from an emotional and intellectual point of view. He felt he would enjoy meeting his father to swop details and share experiences and that it was important to take it all gradually or it would be too emotionally disruptive, with the danger of a sort of burnout in the relationship, if done too quickly.

Before he could start this exercise, he had to find his natural mother. It was to be a satisfactory meeting for both.

Space permits only the highlights of his detailed report to be included.

Of particular concern to him were the conflicting results from using International Directory Enquiries and an internal (US) directory. This was because his father's name and address when tried through International Directory Enquiries was said not to be listed, but the person who was by then helping him in the USA had located him via the local directory.

This is a warning not to take the word of a person in authority as final; one member lost the chance to meet her father in this way when at seventeen she accepted from International Directory Enquiries no one by his name (quite an unusual one) was listed. It was not until she joined TRACE early in 1991 and was advised to at least try to find a relative that she learned differently. Her uncle in South Dakota told her that the father had died only within the last two years. From him she was able to reach her father's widow and through her the son he had adopted by an earlier marriage. He is so delighted to find his beloved father's blood relative, he wanted to send her a ticket to come to him in Arizona and is threatening, in the nicest possible way, to keep her there for ever. So she has achieved a partial happy ending.

To return to 'Paul's' story. He had great praise for the genealogical organisations: 'In general they are intelligent, enthusiastic and very knowledgeable in tracing family connections and, of course, they are not bound by official restrictions.' This is a very important point to remember for any reader about to embark on a search.

'Paul' arrived at TRACE via NORCAP who assist people in the adoption triangle. They send children known to have GI fathers to TRACE. 'The guides and newsletters they [NORCAP] provide were an enormous help when I was searching for my natural mother.' He joined TRACE in September 1987 after receiving some conflicting information from an Air Force historian. This is another warning that one must continue to explore all avenues of information and not rely on just one.

The greatest advantage in this case was to have the home state as a starting point. 'Paul' wrote to the head postmaster of Charleston, West Virginia, with a request for addresses 'listing my target surname'. He also found names of family history researchers in the USA specialising in West Virginia.

The postmaster sent 'Paul' a list of names and addresses of target surnames and the researcher who had agreed to help made contact with his target but did not reveal his telephone number or address to 'Paul'. After two weeks, 'Paul' thought it would help matters along if he explained that his name was changed (through adoption) and that this could be causing his target not to recognise a possible connection. This is worth bearing in mind for anyone in a similar situation since it is what caused the original misunderstanding between David C. from Glamorgan and his father in Tennessee.

'Paul' had yet to reveal to his researcher that there was a family connection and after some time had elapsed he telephoned me to discuss how to deal with the delay. I suggested that the time had come to tell his helper the truth. He took the advice in the hope that she would agree to act as intermediary and enclosed some photographs so they could be used as his introduction.

This proved to be the breakthrough that was needed. He received a short note: 'I am the person you are trying to contact.' He was instructed to write through a company PO box.

Like so many of these children who want to know as much about their fathers as quickly as possible, 'Paul' undertook to analyse his father's handwriting from a book on graphology. He then wrote a 'this is me' letter which produced a reserved reply, not wanting to discuss the past but accepting it by saying: 'It is quite possible I am your biological father.' Some family and business information was added and a request for more pictures. 'Paul' noted that it was signed by the man and his wife with their first names which he took as an encouraging sign.

This was to be followed at Christmas with pictures and a card which he rated as 'very warm and friendly' with a message looking forward to developing a relationship – exactly what 'Paul' had hoped for. A series of 'getting to know you' telephone calls began, then 'Paul' received one from his father's wife which was more serious.

'When I heard he was ill, I actually went into physical shock, although my mind was cool, calm and analytical, my body was shaking uncontrollably. My prime reaction was a selfish one. I felt cheated. I had tracked the man across thousands of miles and thirty-eight years. Now my ultimate goal of meeting him seemed to have slipped from my grasp.'

When his father recovered from a serious operation, 'Paul' knew he had to see him as soon as possible. This was accomplished in May 1991.

'I was welcomed as a true member of the family. I met uncles, aunts, cousins, nephews, nieces and, of course, a brother and sister. I had a surprise birthday party, tourist trips, tours of ancestors' towns, and a mixture of quiet, intimate times and loud fun times. I loved the place and the people and believe a long-term relationship has been forged.

'We spent a marvellous week together full of happiness and optimism. That alone seems like a miracle from what was expected in December 1990. The bond between my family has been made and will continue.'

'Jane' came to her significant decision in 1972.

'I became particularly aware of the gaping hole in my knowledge of my – and therefore my children's – heredity. I decided to ask my adoptive parents if they knew anything about my natural parents. Unfortunately, all they could tell me was that my father was an American soldier and that my maternal grandfather was a KC. Neither of these pieces of information helped me much, though I was intrigued to think that I had an American father.

'In 1977, as a result of much research using official records including those at St Catherine's House, electoral registers and copies of *Who Was Who*, I managed to find information about my grandfather. Then, working my way back chronologically, I traced details of various other members of the family. I also managed to see the contents of my original adoption file and realised that my mother had, in fact, been turned out of her home – "Neck and crop" was the expression used – when expecting another baby. This baby, whose father was not my father and who was born eighteen months before me, had been given up for adoption at birth on the insistence of my mother's parents.

'Since my adoption my mother had married another man and emigrated to the States. It seemed to me, reading between the lines, that a personal approach to the immediate family would probably be distinctly unwelcome.

'I then began to concentrate on trying to trace my mother's first child who had been adopted in 1944, which I succeeded in doing in 1988 by contacting the General Register Office in Titchfield. When we actually made contact she gave me the sad news that our mother had died of cancer – aged thirty-six – in 1958. I can only feel great pity for her plight. She died in hospital and was buried in county ground, her grave unmarked because of her reduced circumstances.

'This grave now has a headstone, my sister and I having arranged for one to be placed in 1989 as near as possible to the exact spot where she was buried.

'I have to say that it is this part of my research that I find hardest to swallow. I know that my mother has been described as wayward – it is quite probable that she was – but to have died an obviously painful and lonely death in these circumstances when her family in England were living in material comfort and security seems to me to be so tragic. This, however, was the end of my search for my mother. I then decided to search for my father.

'When, in 1977, I had originally visited the adoption agency through which I was adopted I had been intrigued to have it confirmed that my father was, indeed, an American soldier posted to the UK during the war. I also deduced from his name that he was Jewish, which intrigued me even more. However, the only information I had about him, apart from his name and age, was the fact that my mother had been hoping to marry him.

'The search for him seemed even more impossible than the one for my mother had been. I did go through some US directories at the American Embassy and also looked at microfiche copies of many more at a library in London, but it was like looking for a needle in a haystack.

'I tried another tack. Some time before I had been given the name of someone in the United States (who had helped others in similar searches) but I had assumed that with so little information about my father they would not be able to help me. I was wrong, and this person managed to discover that there had only been one GI of my father's name and age on active service during the war posted to the UK. However, the delight of discovering this fact was quickly counteracted by the fact that he had died three years before, in 1985. As his wife was still alive I decided that I could pursue my search no further, not knowing how much – if anything – she knew.

'All I could do was visit my father's grave which I did during a visit to the States in 1989, when I also visited my mother's grave.

'On this visit I discovered that my father's wife had died

earlier in 1989. After this, I felt that other members of his family might now be less perturbed by an approach. With the help of a little more research through public records in the States and also help from an American friend in New York, who acted as intermediary, I made an approach to someone who I thought was probably my half-sister.

'She was, and responded with great warmth. She was able to tell me that our father had been a good and loving father to her. He was also a keen amateur singer (perhaps that is where I get my passionate love of music from?) and I am likely to find out more from her about him and his ancestors who came originally from Russia at the beginning of this century.

'My half-sister's first and very touching suggestion when I spoke to her initially was that I should come to New York at Christmas time and she would get tickets for us to see the New York City ballet perform *The Nutcracker*.

'Having reached the end of my search I feel I have done as much as could be expected. I know a bit more about my father but, sadly not as much as I would have liked to know about my mother. I shall never know the circumstances of their romance but I have thought a lot about it and can easily understand two people being thrown together in such frightening and uncertain times as the last war. What I have discovered has made me, on occasions, feel terribly sad – particularly as far as my mother is concerned. But at least I have gone as far as I can in finding out the truth. I freely acknowledge that, since both parents are dead, I have never had a chance to develop any negative feelings about their part in events. I certainly feel that my mother has paid enough without more criticism being poured on her. I do have mixed feelings about the searching process even though I would do the same again.

'I feel that it is essential for adoptees to know as much as possible about the truth of their natural origins and this is now generally accepted, although in some cases the discoveries made must be extremely unsettling.

'I am not sure how often the results of a reunion are as immediately fulfilling as anticipated. In my experience the bondings one has in life are built up over a period of time. I have to admit, though, that I do feel a pang of envy each time I hear a story of a happy and fulfilling reunion of a child and parent and think what might have been.

'While the desire to search was there, it was obsessive; now the search is over, I can relax. I am also very happy that I can now confidently link myself with my roots, even though certain attitudes preclude a formal link.'

Leone W. is another example of persistence and, in her case, refusal to accept rejection. She had grown up with a different name from her half-siblings, knew it was her own father's but had been told he was dead. 'Even on my wedding day, not one of the family mentioned my dad and I so wished I'd had my own dad to walk me down the aisle like my friends.'

It was not until after her two daughters were born that the subject of her father came up again, casually, in conversation, and she finally learned that it was at his insistence she had carried his name.

After she joined TRACE she was one of the few members who turned up at the GI brides reunion in Southampton in 1986 hoping there would be someone there who might be able to help her. She took the opportunity to visit the town library which, as has been mentioned, holds a very good selection of US phone books.

'We got several phone numbers on fiche from Sioux City, Omaha and Nebraska with the "Sailer" name. Over the weeks, I wrote to every address I'd found. Several people replied. If they were not relations, they gave me more addresses to write to.

'I had a reply from an Archie Sailer in Minnesota. He said my letter brought back happy memories of England. He was stationed in Liverpool during the war. He was in the USAF but did not think he was any relation to my dad who was called Arthur Leo Sailer [and had been in the US Navy].

Through writing to so many different people with this name, Leone was recommended to try to trace the deceased part of the family as there are no laws preventing divulgement of such information.

This is a tip worth remembering, but it does not apply in New

York which we have discovered is a 'closed' state. There it would be as well to turn to a genealogical society.

Leone contacted one in Sioux City because that was the town on the label that had accompanied the gifts which had been sent from America in her childhood.

'After several false starts with the wrong families I managed to get an obituary of my grandmother which listed many other family names. One, "Fejfar", being my grandmother's maiden name. There were no addresses but they all seemed to originate from South Dakota or near a place called Utica.'

This was to be the final clue she needed to get an address which she was certain was her father's.

'I wrote on numerous occasions but never had any reply. I traced a telephone number through International Directory Enquiries and was told by the person I phoned that he had never been in England. So, at this stage, he didn't want to know me and I had no way then of verifying whether I had found him.'

Life had to go on and Leone's mother was still very hostile to the idea of her finding her father. Then she died. For a while, everything was abandoned. 'Then, in 1989, I decided as I was the only child, I would go to America and confront that person I was sure was my real father.'

She and her husband flew into Minneapolis, rented a car and made their first stop on the journey to see Archie Sailer who had befriended Leone since that first letter had arrived at his home. 'He checked his family tree and although there were a lot of the same names as my ancestors, none seemed to tie up with the ages etc.'

They proceeded with their journey, stopping at Yankton in North Dakota for a meal. There, drawn into conversation by people who had probably never heard such soft West country accents before, they were persuaded to tell their story.

When Leone mentioned her grandmother's name, she was told there were local people who shared it. At the town's genealogical society, someone found two addresses for them. 'The first, Bill

Fejfar, invited us in, but could not help. However, he said his uncle who was the second address had traced his family tree way back.'

When they visited this man he went through his papers and found the name 'Otille Fejfar' – Leone's grandmother. Not only that, but this man knew her father and through him she learned he had no other children.

It was then she confessed who she really was which took her host by surprise. This made her his relation too as he was her father's cousin. 'He and his wife went so far as to say if after confronting my father he rejected me, they would adopt me as their daughter.' She set off determined to meet her father.

'We found the bungalow and met his wife outside walking their dog. We knew her from the photos shown to us by Bob; she was his second wife. We said we would like to see Arthur Leo. She wanted to know who we were but we said she had better find out from her husband. As soon as he saw me we were invited in and welcomed. He said he had been expecting us. We then stayed with them for a week and found out the reasons for the rejections etc. I am now fully restored into the family and we are planning for them to visit us in England.'

Leone and her husband showed a great deal of courage in pursuing this search to the end. However, *it is an exercise to be taken with a great deal of care. We have known of cases where the reaction was violent..*

Like Leone, Lesley from Yorkshire had known since she was a child that her father was an American. He had been in the Air Force. 'I was excited and expected every plane overhead to be him returning.' She had wanted to find him from the age of fourteen but when at nineteen she went to the States as a nanny, she decided things were best left alone. However, at the age of forty-three she realised that if she delayed any longer it would definitely be too late.

The American Embassy gave her some addresses to follow up which included not only the National Personnel Records Center in St Louis who had a standard reply form for those presenting insufficient details, but the Veterans' Administration office in Sacramento. They informed her that her father had died in Florida in 1967. The alternative now was to find some relatives.

'The only luck I had then was a family of Rosenblatts but the details were wrong. Later, the Air Force Locater Services told me that Major, not Captain, Rosenblatt died 1st December, 1967. No other details. Just as I was beginning to wonder which information was correct, the National Personnel Records Center wrote to say my father died 23rd November, 1957.

In case this appears confusing to the reader, it must be explained that if forms sent by the St Louis office are filled in with the appropriate information, plus proof of paternity such as the GI's name on their birth certificate, in the past they have been known to respond in a helpful way.

For those who argue they have not received such assistance, it could be because they did not fill in the form well enough to meet the approval of the clerk in charge. There seems no precise procedure that one can recommend and in too many cases it does seem to be the mood of the person receiving the mail that day! The change to the Invasion of Privacy act in relation to GIs has altered their attitude. But bear in mind that the more details you supply, the quicker they can help you.

While Lesley waited for copies of her father's birth and death certificates, one of the 'friends' of TRACE in California made some enquiries which resulted in her making contact with some siblings. 'I found out that my father had died in Miami, Florida, in 1967 and left behind three sons and three daughters.' She was able to talk to a brother who was their father's namesake and he gave her some details about him.

Their father had divorced his wife when he returned from the war, then when he married again his new family had taken him over completely. This has left Lesley with a divided set of half-siblings. So far she has only met those on the Californian side of America. She was also able to visit her father's grave.

There was a big reunion of cousins round the pool while she was there and Lesley now feels satisfied she has established the American half of her identity.

This need to fully find themselves is what drives most of these people on. It becomes even more difficult if they have grown up assuming their father is dead, and harder to take when they discover had they started their search earlier he would have been found alive.

Ann B. of Plymouth grew up assuming her father was dead because that was what his CO had told her family when they tried to find out his place of transfer.

'All I had was his name, rank and number. I didn't know where in the States he was from; my mother remembered something about California [it is possible he trained there]. I wrote to every County recorder in California and it was the one in Keen County that passed it to the Veterans' Administration office.

All these letters were written in a businesslike manner and carefully signed with her initial so as not to indicate her sex. They said she had known 'Mr Newborough' during the war and would like to make contact with him again.

'In July 1985, I received a letter from the Veterans' Administration office informing me of my father's date of birth and date of death. With that he became a real person but within seconds I was mourning his death.

'My father's VA file had been located in Cleveland, Ohio, this pointed me in a new direction. From Ohio I managed to get his death certificate and this gave me a great deal of information which led to the area of Lorain where I found my uncle's telephone number.

'I was to find out that my father was born in West Virginia where most of the family still live. They were originally a farming family and descendants of the Cherokee Indians. When my father died he was living in Elymira, Ohio, where his daughter and son lived. He was a factory worker in an air conditioning unit and only fifty-three when he died.'

Ann was one of the few lucky ones who were partly compansated for not meeting their fathers by being able to know their American grandmother. Hers was the classic lady sitting on a rocking chair on an open porch.

From her, Ann learned the unhappy news that her father had been killed while driving under the influence of drink – he was in fact, an alcoholic.

'Grandma said she knew why he drank: there was something on his mind. He did talk about the girl in England; he never forgot her. In fact the year before he died, he had said he was coming back to find her.

'Even now, that makes me cry, for he would have found her still living in the same village. She was divorced, he was a widower and I was looking for a father.'

It was through her uncle that Ann made the initial contact with her family and it was arranged for her to go over to meet them:

'I arrived at Charleston airport feeling like Alice in Wonderland. My aunt and uncle were beaming all over their faces. My uncle held me so tightly, I thought he would break my ribs. He didn't say much, he just wept and said he was "sure as hell" glad I'd found them. Then, a couple of days later, when I was having a meal with them I said something about me being a guest and he said, "You're not a visitor, you're family" and I felt a very happy lady.'

Ann was to find that she got on better with her half-brother than with his sister. The woman had led a typical, sheltered, small-town American life and probably couldn't understand how she could be related to this smart, 'city' gal. However, she must have empathised with her; she gave Ann their father's identity tag: 'Which he must have worn when he was over here during the war. This means so much to me.'

Later, Ann paid for her half-brother to visit England which he loved: 'But the only time he was really happy was in a pub. The responsibility was too great so we suggested he went back home which he was ready to do. He said he started to drink after Vietnam.'

They did visit places their father had been to in England. One of them was the large white house about a quarter of a mile from where her mother had lived:

'As a child I used to look longingly at this place where he had been stationed and wonder what he was like. It was amazing to stand in the drive with my brother. I was lent my father's photograph album when I was in America and found a photograph of that house. I had still questioned, when I found the Newboroughs, if I had the right family. I was terrified in case I had the wrong ones. But when I found that photograph it was proof that I had the right man.

'Someone asked me what I felt like after visiting my father's grave. I replied that I had spent forty years climbing Mount Everest. At his grave, I just put the flag on the top!'

ELEVEN

I'm Making Tortillas for Tea

'I've finally had a father tell me he loves me,' says Diane W. from Somerset. She had returned from a rapturous reception in April 1991. 'He said he loved my mother but she didn't love him enough to go to America.'

Diane visited her father and family in a Texas border town. There she was to discover that she was the darkest of all his children. 'A woman who passed me in the street there said in Spanish, she recognised me as the first-born.' Diane came home thrilled with her Mexican heritage.

Nothing will ever replace for all the people in her position, those magic words they long to hear. For one man who finally found a telephone number to match his father's last address there was instant disappointment. His father had moved but the occupants of the house promised to pass on to him the fact that someone from England had telephoned. This led to an early a.m. conversation:

'Why are you looking for me?'
'So that I can call you Dad.'
'Hello, Son,' the GI said.

As has been seen from some of the case histories in this book, these people are profoundly changed by all aspects of the experience of tracking down their father's whereabouts. It is not all joyous; even if it reaches a successful conclusion, they can plummet from a terrific high to such a frightening low that they need counselling.

Heather from chapter one says:

'The last few years have been an emotional see-saw and I
sometimes wish I had never started the search. It is confusing
to live life in the wrong order and hard on the family. However,
time passes and puts things in perspective. I feel a more complete
person now. I'm glad I know who I am.'

Others try to hide the fact that they are disappointed that the
real father has destroyed a romantic image they have carried
for too long a time. I understand. When I hear the locations
they are off to visit, I often suffer twinges of concern. Should
I say, 'Don't go, you are heading for a terrible disappointment'?
Of course not – I would be ignored. Even 'Take care' would
do nothing to diminish their excitement. I limit my advice to
suitable clothing: full thermal underwear, if it is winter and they
are going to places like Nebraska! Casual clothing wherever else
they go. There is rarely a need to get 'dressed up'. Then, I cross
my fingers and sometimes offer the phone number of a 'friend'
on a 'just in case' basis.

It is impossible to warn them to go into this emotionally charged
moment with an open mind. Their father was their goal, often only
achieved after years of searching. They do not at once recognise
that it is rarely only 'Dad' they are on their way to meet; his
wife and other children's reaction will have some bearing on
what ensues.

Added to that, his lifestyle, residence or attitudes can be very
different and hard to contend with after the initial hugs and tears.
'Dad' is an American, a 'foreigner' in every sense of the word.
The culture shock they experience can be similar to that felt by
their mothers' peers – the GI brides. This can overtake the initial
euphoria fast.

'Autumn' went off too full of hope. First, in August 1990, I
received a letter which said:

'I listened to the soft southern accent of a gentleman. I felt the
warmth and sincerity in his voice and his many regrets about
the past. I can still hear his voice in my head; I can't take it

in that today, I spoke to and heard my father . . . I've walked around in a daze since putting the phone down.'

This was followed in September by another letter reporting a phone call:

'My father is wonderful. All I could have ever wished for. He is sensitive, loving and such a gentleman. I can't tell you how happy I am. My dad has been baby pig minding. Great idea! He is so apologetic about the poverty and not being able to get back here, and how he tried year after year. I can't make him understand that I don't give a hoot about money or what he did for a living. I just want him and now it's all happening. I'm still on cloud nine.'

When she told me her destination in the States, I wondered whether to warn her about how different it would be from where she lived, then kept silent. She had to discover like the rest of them that there are more families in America like in *Roseanne*, living modestly and working to pay bills, than the Colbys of *Dynasty*. Neither is all of America like Disneyworld; there are still a lot of 'red-neck' hillbillies living very limited lives.

So, 'Autumn' went off with her husband to spend Christmas deep in the country. I received a postcard with a cryptic message: 'Having a trip I don't believe.'

When she returned, she wrote to say it had been a total disaster: 'I would like my story to be told to serve as a warning to others of how you can sometimes open a can of worms.' It wasn't so much that her father was living in a trailer in the back of beyond but she couldn't deal successfully with certain aspects of his lifestyle, especially a fanatical attitude to religion and casual approach to shooting wildlife. It is not easy for most British people to adjust to the sight of a dead deer proudly draped across the bonnet of a car as a trophy of a hunting trip. It is also wiser if one can remain objective about diverse views on religion and *keep the mouth firmly shut*.

However, her father was not about to allow his many years of hope flounder in the sea of her disappointment. He ignored the unhappy letter she wrote to him when she was back in England

and, fortunately, since then she has seen the sense of making a return visit.

Some people have found that it takes a second visit to really fit that missing piece of their personal jigsaw into place comfortably. They also need to decide if their intense love affair with America is real enough to up sticks and go and live there.

Frank H. who appeared in the chapter on stepfathers has told me to refer any would-be immigrants to him – speaking as the voice of experience!

Regardless of how the reunion is accomplished or whether it is the father or his family who fill in the spaces which have been empty all their lives, especially if they were adopted, reunited children acquire different personae – a fact they greet with relief:

> 'Staking a claim on one's heredity should not be seen as being aggressive or menacing. It is merely that the truth of my heredity is what I have discovered plus experiences I have had – *not* what was unconsciously "manufactured" for me during the years of my ignorance [she was adopted]. What I am is: half Russian-Jewish-American and half Anglo-Irish and not what I assumed I was meant to be for twenty-seven years of my life, i.e., one hundred per cent English. I am passionate and emotional and couldn't possibly erase those traits from my character even if I wanted or tried to. I have felt many times in my life that to be phlegmatic was normal and to be me was therefore to be the opposite. I no longer feel that.'

'Jane' has learned all of this from finding her half-sister in New York.

Sue K. who now lives in Pennsylvania has also been filled in, in her case, by a large, welcoming group of relatives:

> 'I don't know any of the other "War Bastards" but it's so difficult to tell people what it means to find your family. They love the story, of course, I mean, it's so damned entertaining, but I don't feel they really understand what it means in the way I feel about things, the way I approach life.

'When I first learned that he had died, that I'd never hug my "daddy", Joel [her husband] said, "You mustn't be disappointed." Truth be known, I wasn't. I was so happy I'd found the missing link. But now, a few months down the road, I'm finally realising all I missed by not finding him sooner. I look at those pictures and I look at those pictures. It's almost as though they are part of my history now.'

In general, people are able to take the philosophical view that the search, like marriage, is for better or worse. What comes hardest is rejection as 'Howard' has found:

'What he has done by lying is more hurtful than if he had told me straight instead of stringing me along. Building my hopes up then dragging me down. I have put a brave face on the matter but deep down, it's tearing me apart – it's like having your heart torn out. I just can't believe any person could treat their own blood like this. It's like being kicked in the teeth. I feel more sorry for my father than bitter. I wrote this straight from the heart and hope it helps you finish my story.

PS: I still live in hope that one day he might have a change of heart.'

All I can personally say to this man in Colorado is – please do!

One of the other TRACE members did discover that rejection is not always final.

In 'Toni's' case, the Veterans' Administration official who had been helping her made the telephone call which convinced her father that he should stop ignoring the letters and photographs that 'Toni' continued to send: 'My story has a happy ending. My father called me. We had a very tearful talk. He's coming over to stay with us.' When he did, he was delighted to find his daughter and he were very much alike. Needless to say, he was doubly enchanted with his grandchildren.

I have often been asked what right I have to encourage people to set out on this quest. I point out that they have rights too and sometimes a pressing need on behalf of their own children to complete their medical history.

I accept it can cause upset and disruption, however careful and tactful the approach may be, but their conception was an act between two people. They have the right to know who both of them were.

What has become obvious is that not all the fathers deserted the British mothers deliberately. If Mum wouldn't join him in America, what could he do?

That doesn't mean that they forgot the girl they left behind. Alan's parents' late marriage is a classic example of the GIs who never forgot their British sweethearts.

Other men (innocent or ignorant as they were on arrival of the British way of life), enjoying the relaxed rules pertaining to their religion – such as the fact that in service, Catholic men could eat meat on Friday and Jews pork – may have seen a marriage here as an extension of this.

Their child armed with a copy of the marriage certificate and birth certificate bearing his name can come as a nasty shock. It may account for the silence of some after they are tracked down.

Fortunately, they are balanced by the number of fathers who have said: 'I'm so glad you have found me.' Some had even employed a private investigator to try to find them. For those who had paid maintenance, they had also left vital clues to find them from the paperwork.

The American wife has received 'mixed notices' from the British children. They go from understandable hostility to freely offered friendship. The latter more especially true if she married the GI after the affair.

American siblings too, are varied in their response: 'What do you want?' was the cold question in a letter from one half-sister. It is sometimes hard to convince these people that the need is emotional not monetary.

Certain circumstances have produced an impasse after the fathers were found – not always financial. Contrary to what might be thought there are still a large number of people in the USA who are apprehensive of flying. Many servicemen from World War II will not consider the alternative of crossing by ship because they retain unpleasant memories of the wartime voyage. There are also some who do not realise that there is a difference in cultural attitudes and fear the family will come after them with a shotgun for what they did to their daughter!

Anyone tempted to take off blindly across the United States in the hope of stumbling, miraculously, upon their missing dad was soon to discover they should have had a starting point, preferably a town. Without preparation or planning, help was not easy to find. With the few exceptions mentioned, they received an impersonal, 'stick to the rules' reception from authorities.

The people who benefited the most in their search, were the ones with an understanding partner; just as well because we had a few marriages swamped by the impenetrable jungle of paperwork and frustration that is almost inevitable in the greater number of cases.

Every cliche in fiction became fact in the writing of this book – from wayward daughters and the 'never darken my doorstep again' scenario to last-minute bedside dashes to dying fathers. One daughter discovered that her father had been living in England for many years and the Gulf War raised the distinct possibility that World War II GIs had British and American grandsons fighting side by side.

Throughout some of the searches within the TRACE organisation, Sophia Byrne and I found we were often acting as surrogate mothers. Along with the counselling and comforting were arguments and sometimes the need to bully them into further action. One classic case involved Sophia suggesting the one last try be a burrow through the local authority records. This was not only to result in someone finding his father of eighty, but Mum being proposed to by telephone. Off she went to marry the man who had obviously been the love of her life.

This was never the general purpose of TRACE. Women looking for the wartime boyfriend were discouraged because of the havoc they could cause.

There was another unusual link-up which was not of our making. Towards the end of 1990, Lesley, having established herself with the Californian half of her family, came home to

169

nurse a very sick mother who died soon after her return. Around the same time, in conversation with someone whose mother had also recently died, she discovered the lady was the child of a GI. In what must be the most unique wake ever organised, they decided to go together to see the film *Memphis Belle* and relive their parents' romances which had also taken place around an American Air Force base.

Even before the court action made it legal for the various American Veterans' groups to assist people looking for GI fathers, TRACE had already discovered that not all those officials were that hard hearted. One applicant found, along with the official letter citing the Invasion of Privacy law as reason they could not respond to his request, a crumpled piece of paper on which his father's address was written!

What continues for these children of the GIs is the uncertainty of how they will be received. This has made many hesitate – some literally on their father's doorstep. They feel they cannot deal with the possible rejection which would destroy their dream and so back away.

That dream of finding the GI has already been picked up by the next generation. There is a steady increase in letters asking for help in finding their American grandpa. This one arrived in July 1990:

Dear Sir/Madam,
My name is Ailsa Fiona Sanders. I am twelve years old. I wish help in tracing my grandfather in the hope of corresponding. My grandfather's name is William Henry Sanders, his rank is sergeant in the US Army. His serial number is 6279171. I'm not sure when he was born but he will be in his late 70s now.
My father, Michael David Sanders, was born 21.1.45. He enquired about him but never succeeded. I wish to try and find out all about him as I have no grandfather and all I wish for is to succeed in my wish.
Thank you very much,
Ailsa Sanders.

The number indicated two possible states. In each case the Governor wrote back to say there was no trace of the GI.

Then, Ailsa's father suggested to me that it might be Oklahoma. He wasn't there either, then sadly Ailsa was to learn that her grandfather had died in April 1951 in Amarillo, Texas.

This GI was one who wanted to take the baby back with him to America, but the mother had preferred to dump him in a home which gave Ailsa's dad a disruptive childhood. More's the pity we couldn't have provided him with a happy ending.

TWELVE
A Few Last Words from Those Still Searching

Someone in Hertfordshire prefers to remain nameless:

'There is hardly a day goes by that I do not think of my father. What does he look like? Do I look like him? Does my temper come from him? Why doesn't he try to find me? I feel somehow incomplete having never met this man – how can I ever feel whole? If only I could see him, even just once to satisfy my own curiosity. To say, "Well, here I am, what do you think of me, your daughter? How about your granddaughter and grandson, you don't know them and you are missing out on two wonderful children."

'If my father had brought me up, would I have been so very different from the person I am now? How will I ever know?

'I pray to God that one day I will find my father and that he is a good man deep down. Then, this huge question mark above my head, the feeling in my heart, and the answers to all my questions will be gone and I can get on with my life, knowing I am complete.'

Michael L. is a businessman in Essex who was always left on the outside looking in on the children of his mother's later marriage. He offers the following observation:

'In many ways I have been very lucky in life with a good deal of success, particularly in my career. Deep inside I have always had a feeling of insecurity and I am sure if I had had the real

172

love and attention of my own father, life and love would have
developed for me in a more natural path and I would have
been able to trust others much more than I do.

'Maybe I am too old now but if I were to meet him I know it
would give me the one and only thing I want and still need.

'I believe he loved me very much and thought that love was
returned by the life my mother chose for me. If only he knew
how wrong he was.'

Elaine H. from her vantage point of now being a loved member
of her American family offers this advice:

'I would say to people searching, don't be sorry for the rest of
your life – carry on, whilst you can. There are times I wanted
to give up but through sheer determination I kept going and it
was all worth it in the end. I have a lot to look forward to in
life, it makes up for the early unsettled years. You can only be
rejected or accepted, so carry on.'

Obviously, no one ceased in their efforts while this book was being
prepared which is why I offer no apologies for the postscripts that
follow in which, in some cases, fate took a determined hand, and
television played its part.

LWT's 6 o'clock Live contacted me to see if we could arrange
a Christmas reunion. Tina of Slough, who had poured her life
across fourteen pages of a letter after she had found her father,
was willing to let her meeting with him be a public event. As it
happens, I saw him first as a silver-haired man came up behind
her as she waited at Heathrow Airport. Because she was holding a
present for him, her hands were not free to hug him tightly, so
this is a lesson for everyone to learn! Don't carry anything when
you run to meet your father!

Tina has now gone from being the adored, only daughter of
adopted parents to being part of a large family of siblings of
varying ages to match her father's three marriages. The next step
is to meet them all.

Television played a hand in what happened to Jennifer of Kent
who had been adopted but was terribly bothered by not knowing

her background. Her husband just happened to come home for lunch the day I was on BBC's *Daytime Live* discussing TRACE. He had the presence of mind to tape this for his wife. This led to her joining TRACE and being given the necessary help and advice on how to proceed.

She had the advantage of an unusual last name which was easier to pick out in the telephone book. From the letters she wrote she was to learn that her father had died but waiting for her in Texas was a collection of aunts, uncles and, most important, a grandmother of ninety-eight who said: 'If you want loving, we'll love you.' It appears she had wanted her son to marry this British girl and when he refused, had wanted her to come to them in America with the baby .

Because her father had treated her mother so badly, when she was told by Jennifer about her adventure in Texas she decided to break off her contact. 'She wanted me back in the past again as it was not doing her health any good as I reminded her of someone she never wanted to think of again.'

Regardless, Jennifer feels:

'I've learned a lot about myself through finding my mother and my father's family. Now I know who I take after and I have a history of my own. Although not everything worked out well, I am very glad I continued through the setbacks and finally made it. My American family are such lovely people, it makes me sad that I have not known them longer, particularly my grandmother. She died not long after I came back.'

One success story came through delayed action. 'Penny' had applied for membership to TRACE after reading a 'Precious Moments' letter in *Bella* magazine. A year later, leafing through papers prior to starting work on this book, I became curious as to why she had not returned her application form and discovered it had never arrived through the post.

When she sent her details I learned that her parents had been married, but as her mother had ignored the letters that her father had sent, demanding they join him in the States he divorced her for 'repeated mental cruelty'.

These papers provided 'Penny' with his home town, so I

suggested she try International Directory Enquiries to see if he was still resident there. When she was given the number of someone with the same name she took the plunge and telephoned.

What she did not know was that this was her half-brother's number *but* her father was visiting from his retirement home in Florida and it was he who picked up the receiver.

'I'm very glad I phoned. It's all a bit too much to take in and I have very mixed emotions, I felt nothing for him before and now I've spoken to him, I don't know what I feel. I didn't tell him much other than he has another two grandchildren. He sounded like a nice person. I will write and take things from there.'

With this, 'Penny' began to make plans to visit Florida and meet him!

A wonderful last-minute addition should put heart into those suffering rejection or perhaps encourage them to try, 'just one more time'.

Linda B. from Essex, who opened chapter four but was too miserable to wish to be identified, only joined TRACE in January 1991. She had been left in limbo by her father's denial when she telephoned in late February. But, encouraged by her husband, she had written a letter of explanation and began to watch the post in the hope he would reconsider and reply.

In early April he rang her to explain that her call had come as a shock and an unbelievable surprise. He had been in such a state that he had not written down her address, so it was with great relief that he received the follow-up letter which arrived in March.

He proceeded to fill her in on the full story: he had been married when he met her mother. When he heard that a baby was due, he had written to ask his wife for a divorce. Her response was to suggest he bring the baby home with him but Linda's mother would not agree to this. Subsequently, she married a man who adopted the baby.

The GI was not fully informed and, when notified, assumed that the adoption meant the baby had gone to another family and he would never see her again. This is not the first time such a situation has occurred when the child approaches the father. The confusion is added to when, like David C. of Glamorgan, they have an unrecognisable name.

Linda's father made it clear she will be made very welcome by him and his wife and, undoubtedly, they will have met before the publication date of this book.

Two final notes:

If this book has stirred up a few happy memories or possibly touched a conscience or two from the clues I tried to drop discreetly, please get in touch with me and I will try to point you in the direction of your child, grandchildren and, in several cases, great-grandchildren.

And

Because 1992 is the 50th Anniversary of the arrival of those hordes of GIs on Britain's shores, it would be a good idea if the various groups in the UK involved in finding GI fathers would start to cross-reference so that no one is unwittingly left out or misses the GI looking for his British child.

USEFUL ADDRESSES

Please note that these are the last known addresses. I cannot be responsible if they have since been changed.

ACTION LINE

In the *Miami Herald*. Anne Baumgartner, Editor, has personally offered to help in that area. One Herald Plaza, Miami, FL 33132-1693

AIR FORCE SERGEANTS' ASN

PO Box 31050, Temple Hills, MD 20748

AMERICAN ASSOCIATION OF MINORITY VETERANS

c/o Governor's Office of Veterans' Affairs, Lausche State Office, 615 West Superior Avenue, Cleveland, OH 44114 (For Mexican Americans)

AMERICAN CEMETERIES IN EUROPE

First contact is the American Cemetery, Madingley Road, Coton, Cambridge, CB3 7PH

THE AMERICAN LEGION

PO Box 1055, Indianapolis, IN 46206
(Will forward a letter if the GI is a member. Address your covering letter to the Librarian and Curator)

AMERICAN MERCHANT MARINE VETERANS

905 Cape Coral Parkway, Cape Coral, FL 33904

ARIEL BRUCE AGENCY

6 Regent Square, London, WC1 8HZ

THE ARMY TIMES, THE NAVY TIMES and THE AIR FORCE TIMES

Are now all at the same address: 6993 Commercial Drive, Springfield, VA 22159

THE BULGE BUGLE

Is the official publication of veterans of the Battle of the Bulge. Members have the Ardennes Campaign Battle Star dated 7th Dec. 1944.
PO Box 11129, Arlington, VA 22110-2129

BURTONWOOD TIMES

Thomas E. Conley, Editor, 2946 Savannah Court, Waco, TX 75710 (Only useful if the GI was at Burtonwood)

CASUALTY AND MEMORIAL AFFAIRS DIRECTORATE

HQS-DA-D-A-G-PED-F, Room 984, Hoffman Building, 2451 Eisenhower Avenue, Alexandria, VA 22331

DRAFT REGISTER

Atlanta Federal Records Center, 1557 St Joseph Avenue, East Point, Atlanta, GA 30344 (If looking in Georgia)

GEBORENER DEUTSCHER

William Gage, 2300 Ocean Avenue, Brooklyn, NY 11229 (For anyone with German connections)

GENEALOGISTS INC.

Suite 113, 2031 North Broad Street, Lansdale, PA 19446 (For a fee they will send a list of names and addresses of all the individuals in their database with the surnames for which you are searching)

THE GENERAL REGISTRY

PO Box 7, Titchfield, Fareham, Hants, PO15 5RU

HOLBORN REFERENCE LIBRARY

Theobolds Road, London, WC1

ITALIAN AMERICAN WAR VETERANS OF THE US INC.

115 Meridian Road, Youngstown, OH 44509

JEWISH WAR VETERANS OF THE USA

1811 12 Street NW, Washington, DC 20009

KIN QUEST

PO Box 873, Bowling Green Station, New York, NY 10274-0873 (They have access via CompuServe to a national database)

KNIGHTS OF COLUMBIA

One Columbia Plaza, New Haven, CT 06507 (A lot of Catholic Americans are members of this group which is like the Masons)

MEX AM VETS

American GI Forum, Outreach Program, 1521 South Port, Corpus Christi, TX 78415

MILITARY ORDER OF THE PURPLE HEART USA INC.

5413-B Backlick Road, Springfield, VA 22151

NATIONAL ASSOCIATION FOR BLACK VETERANS INC.

3929 North Humboldt Drive, PO Box 11432, Milwaukee, WI 53211-0432

NATIONAL PERSONNEL RECORDS CENTER

9700 Page Blvd, St Louis, MO 63132 (Mark envelope 'do not open in mail room', attn Charles Pellegrini)

NAVAL HISTORICAL CENTER

Washington Navy Yard, Bldg 220, Washington, DC 20375 (If trying to locate which ship a GI was on, give them dates and British port)

THE NEW YORK GENEALOGICAL AND BIBLIOGRAPHICAL SOCIETY

122 East 58th Street, New York, NY 10022 (Will send a list of researchers in the USA. Remember to send them an International Reply Coupon)

NORCAP

(National Association for the Counselling of Adoptees and Parents) 3 New High Street, Headington, Oxford, OX3 7AJ

PUBLIC RECORDS OFFICE

Ruskin Avenue, Kew, Surrey

ROOTS

PO Box 94, Hyde Park, Ontario, NOM 1ZO (For Canadian fathers)

SHAEF COMMUNIQUE

PO Box 42, Fair Haven, NJ 07704 (Only if the GI was in this group)

USEFUL ADDRESSES

TOGETHER AGAIN

Pat Morgan, Editor, 11902 Southlake Drive, Houston, TX 770077 (Ask 'if anyone knows the whereabouts of . . .')

TRACE

Sophia Byrne, Membership Secretary, 11 St Tewdrick's Place, Mathern, Nr Chepstow, Gwent, NT6 6JW

USAF HEADQUARTERS

DPM/DOP, Randolph AFB, TX 78150-6001

US ARMY ENGINEERING SCHOOL

Fort Leonardwood, MO 65473

US ARMY MILITARY INSTITUTE

Carlisle Barracks, PA 17013-5008

US MARINES (RET)

National Personnel Records Center (Marines), 9700 Page Blvd, St Louis, MO 63132-5100

VETERANS' ADMINISTRATION OFFICE

810 Vermont Avenue NW, Washington, DC 20420 (You require a veteran's service number, which will then be sent to the appropriate VA state office if the number is on their lists)

VETERANS' AFFAIRS

Richard Raine, Asst Div. Chief, PO Box 942, Sacramento, CA 94295-0001

VETERANS' ALUMNI ASSOCIATION

Tom Wagner, 309 Long Shadow Lane, Mesquite, TX 75149 ($3

to join; $1 per search. He will pass on a communication if the GI is on his lists. Bear in mind that so far he has 300,000 names, but these include Korean and Vietnam veterans too)

VEHICLE OPERATOR SEARCHES

PO Box 15334, Sacramento, CA 95851-1334

VIRGIL THOMPSON

1029 Center Street, Lima, OH 43801 (Only USAF enquiries)

8TH AIR FORCE HISTORICAL SOCIETY

PO Box 3556, Hollywood, FL 33083

82ND AIRBORNE DIVISION ASSOCIATION

PO Box 1442, Bloomington, IN 47402

82ND AIRBORNE STATIC LINE

PO Box 87518, College Park, GA 30337 (Don Lasen)

82ND AIRBORNE WAR MEMORIAL MUSEUM

Dept Army, Fort Bragg, NC 28307

And an invaluable book:

How to Locate Anyone Who Is or Has Been in the Military Armed Forces Locater Directory by Lt.-Col. Richard S. Johnson, Military Information Enterprises, PO Box 340001, Fort Sam, Houston, TX 78234

I conclude as I do all the newsletters that go out to TRACE members: Good hunting!

A NOTE ON THE AUTHOR

Pamela Winfield was a GI bride who returned to the UK after she
was widowed, and later remarried. *Bye Bye Baby* is her fourth book.
She gives talks on a wide range of subjects, one of which is
the children the GIs left behind. She says her greatest satisfaction
in helping these people has come from finding the families of the men
who were killed in the fighting in Europe. 'These families rarely knew
that a child had been left behind and have been delighted with the
British branch of their family tree.'